Expressive Typography

Expressive Typography
The Word as Image

Kimberly Elam

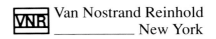 Van Nostrand Reinhold
New York

Copyright © 1990 by Van Nostrand Reinhold

Library of Congress Catalog Card Number 89-16414
ISBN 0-442-23356-6

Printed in the United States of America

Van Nostrand Reinhold
115 Fifth Avenue
New York, New York 10003

Van Nostrand Reinhold International Company Limited
11 New Fetter Lane
London EC4P 4EE, England

Van Nostrand Reinhold
480 La Trobe Street
Melbourne, Victoria 3000, Australia

Nelson Canada
1120 Birchmount Road
Scarborough, Ontario
Canada M1K 5G4

16 15 14 13 12 11 10 9 8 7 6 5 4 3 2 1

Library of Congress Cataloging-in-Publication Data
Elam, Kimberly, 1951-
    Expressive typography: the word as image / Kimberly Elam.
        p. cm.
    Includes Index.
    ISBN 0-442-23356-6
    1. Printing, Pratical—Layout. 2. Type and type-founding.
I. Title.
Z246.E53 1990
686.2'2—dc20   89-16414
                                      CIP

Contents

Preface

This book opens a door on typographic communication that has remained closed for much of the twentieth century. This door has been opened only briefly, by artists, designers, and their works, but it will require many more of each even to begin to explore all that is behind it. But even this glimpse reveals intriguing clues to the past and the present, and a new perspective on the future of typography.

The search for the key to this door began when, as a design practitioner and educator, I began to question the traditional definition of typography, which identified only machine-set letterforms as typographic and excluded all handcraft methods of creating typography, such as handwriting, illustration, and modeling. Why were designers taught to conceptualize and draw images, compose photographs, and design dimensional models but never to apply the same knowledge and techniques to typography? Why was learning typography and visualizing images separated by attitudes and curricular constraints?

To understand both these questions and their answers, I reexamined the past, present, and possible future of typography, and *Expressive Typography* is the result. It is different from most other studies in that its primary focus is on typography.

By bringing together evidence from art, design, architecture, sociology, and technology, *Expressive Typography* offers new insight into modern typography and expands the traditional definition of typography to include all means of creating written language. This expanded definition gives the typographic word the ability to transcend didactic meaning, and recognizes its effective use of space and dimension, thereby becoming an image in itself. It shows that it is possible to combine successfully typography and image, by returning to and acknowledging the recent roots of graphic design in the late nineteenth and early twentieth centuries.

In this book we identify and analyze methods that synthesize image generation with typographic design. We also apply the same learning associated with the visual interpretation and composition of images including photography, illustration, collage, and abstraction, to the interpretation and composition of verbal messages. This collaborative development of the image and typography enables the word to become the image and the image to become the word.

Of particular interest are the works that provoked innovative change during the nineteenth and early twentieth centuries by such fine artists and architects as Jules Chéret, Pierre Bonnard, Alfred Roller, Lucian Bernhard, as well as by Bauhaus visionaries such as Laszlo Moholy-Nagy, El Lissitzky, and Joost Schmidt. The revolutionary transformations of the style, intent, and attitudes toward typography were closely bound to changes in technology, society, and the fine arts. These are the same kinds of changes our world is increasingly experiencing, and the cyclical path of history returns us to these works for renewed revelation and innovation through the work of modern designers.

The chapters that follow examine the roots of—and paths to—expressive typography. Each chapter concludes with experimental work done by design students. Unbound by the constraints and restrictions of budgets, clients, and learned biases, students are able to approach typography with a fresh perspective. The instructors who directed this work have guided their students with both an appreciation of the past and an analytical understanding of the present. The students have responded through their work by presenting a vision of the future.

This book is intended as a resource for further typographic exploration and as a source of visual inspiration. The ideas and techniques it contains represent only some of the many approaches to and methods of creating words as images. But we hope that this book will serve as a valuable starting point in the creation of expressive typography.

Acknowledgments

I am deeply indebted to all of the contributors who so very generously shared their work for this book. Their interest and enthusiasm for this project made it possible.

I would also like to thank the following institutions and people: The Ohio Arts Council, for providing the funding that initiated research; The Ohio State University, Department of Industrial Design, for providing research support; The North Carolina State University, Department of Product and Visual Design, particularly Haig Khachatoorian, Martha Lange, Bill Deere, and P. Lyn Middleton, for sharing their expertise; Patricia A. Moore, for continuous enthusiastic encouragement, editorial assistance, and valuable criticism throughout the project; Philip B. Meggs, for excellent and generous advice and insight into research resources and publishing; and James Molloy, Jan Ostendorf, Dan Shust, and Karine Bielefeld, for organizational and production assistance.

Thanks also to: Lilly Kaufman, Sponsoring Editor at Van Nostrand Reinhold, whose faith in this project, encouragement, and direction made it possible; Paul Lukas, Editorial Supervisor, who thoughtfully guided the production of this project to completion; and Sandra Cohen, for production management.

1.1 Laszlo Moholy-Nagy, *Photogram,* 1922.
International Museum of Photography at the
George Eastman House.

1.2 Laszlo Moholy-Nagy, *Bauhaus Books 14,*
front cover and spine, 1929. Courtesy of the
Bauhaus-Archiv, West Berlin.

Chapter 1
Planar Typography

Planar Typography

All typography exists on the imaginary surface of a plane. Usually this typographic plane is flat, invisible, and is seen from a frontal view such as the typography you are now reading. The planar typography discussed in this chapter, however, differs in that the plane on which it rests shifts and changes position in space. As the plane angles, bends, overlaps, or moves in space, so too does the typography. The concept of planar typography releases words from the flat page, thus allowing them to occupy space and even to have expressive visual connotations.

The planar typography itself is essentially flat and has only a very slight implied dimension that permits letterforms and words to be affected by the principles of perspective. Typographic elements on a plane appear smaller as they recede from the viewer; the edges of these elements converge as they recede; and the closer elements overlap those farther away. Although planes have implied dimension, they are different from three-dimensional typography, discussed in Chapter 4.

The Historical Context: Typography in the Twentieth Century

During the first quarter of the twentieth century, in the midst of a technological, social, and artistic revolution, typography underwent a revolution of its own, in form, composition, and function. Abandoning the embellishment and ornamentation of art nouveau, sans serif type styles became preferred for their simple, legible forms. Movements in fine art, including dadaism, cubism, de stijl, constructivism, futurism, and the Bauhaus school, brought experimentation in asymmetric composition, the visual dynamics of diagonal composition, and the use of abstract compositional elements. Typography became more important than ever before, as words and letterforms were regarded as objective and utilitarian communicative elements, which rapidly began to subordinate or replace the image as the primary visual force. Typography became eminently functional in its role as a visual communicator.

The earlier fine arts medium of photomontage and the documentary medium of photography became powerful tools in the 1920s as designers such as Man Ray, El Lissitsky, Rodchenko, and Laszlo Moholy-Nagy began to experiment with photography as a medium for both art and communication. Some of the first experiments were with photograms, a technique of arranging objects on light-sensitive paper and then exposing the paper with light (**Fig. 1.1**). Later experiments used the more complex medium of photomontage, a technique of making a collage from several photographic images so as to create unexpected visual contrasts.

The camera rapidly became an indispensable tool of visual communication. For example, experiments with space, surface, light, and shadow, as in Moholy-Nagy's *Bauhaus Books 14* cover, were photographed and printed (**Fig. 1.2**).

By the 1920s, improvements in the technology of printing and the quality of printing inks also enabled more experimentation in photographic manipulation. Much finer halftone screens, which are necessary in the print reproduction of a number of tones or values from a single color of ink, became available and facilitated experimentation and the use of more subtle tonal arrangements. Through experiments with photographic printing and photograms, designers found that just as photographs could be manipulated and distorted by the use of light in the darkroom, so too could typographic images. The same photographic techniques that created depth, space, transparency, and movement permitted typographic elements to do the same.

1

1.3 Joost Schmidt, design for an advertisement for Bauhaus wallpaper, ca. 1930. Courtesy of the Bauhaus-Archiv, West Berlin.

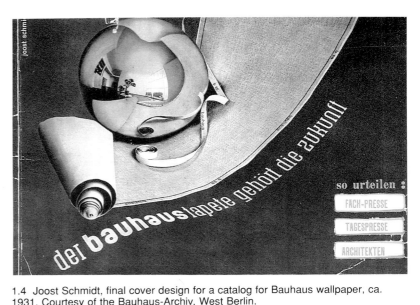

1.4 Joost Schmidt, final cover design for a catalog for Bauhaus wallpaper, ca. 1931. Courtesy of the Bauhaus-Archiv, West Berlin.

Joost Schmidt, first a student and later a teaching master at the Bauhaus, used the Bauhaus experiments in photography and typography in his studies and final cover for a manufacturer of Bauhaus wallpaper. The reflective sphere is symbolic of the new age of technological achievement that was an important part of the Bauhaus philosophy. In Schmidt's first studies, the typography is reflected in the sphere, along with portions of an interior space that combined to form a visual statement about the product and its use, fusing the words and images into a single element **(Fig. 1.3)**. On the final cover the typography and sphere image are separated, probably for reasons of clarity and legibility, but they still join visually to make a cohesive statement **(Fig. 1.4)**.

Perspective Representation

For many centuries artists have been aware of the visual power of perspective drawing and painting, which enables the viewer to perceive dimension and depth. Perspective orders objects and their relative distance from the viewer by changes in size, foreshortening, convergence, transparency and overlapping, color and value, detail and pattern, and focus or texture gradient. The illusory qualities of perspective are what enable the viewer to perceive space and/or dimension on a flat printed page and thus are indispensable to releasing typography from a flat, planar context.

The camera also records dimension in letterforms, objects, or environments and thereby manipulates typography by means of perspective principles. The concept of distance can be explored and heightened by manipulating either the process or the objects in order to control and simulate distance and position in space. Even when using hand-graphic techniques to represent perspective, the camera—and what is learned from visual experiments with the camera—assist the designer in developing typographic compositional images.

Letterforms in Perspective

Letterforms and words seem to adapt well to perspective manipulation. Letterforms have a visual familiarity that is easily retained, and experiments have shown that they remain legible even when severely cropped. That is, the eye is so accustomed to the shapes of letters that generally only a few selected visual clues are needed to recognize them. Such clues are ascenders, descenders, and position on the baseline.

Typographic elements make an excellent subject for perspective experimentation, because their correct position and orientation (in order to be read) are well known. The baseline position is assumed to be either horizontal or vertical for all typography, and so changes are readily recognized and the eye is rapidly reoriented.

The key to understanding typography that is manipulated by perspective is to see the compositional boundaries as the frame of an open window with the potential for limitless space. By regarding the edges of the format as an invisible frame through which lies unlimited space, typographic elements are released from their usual flat, front view plane and are allowed to occupy space and have dimension.

The Perspective Principle of Convergence

The perspective principle of convergence states that parallel edges tend to come together as they recede from the viewer. This principle is a combination of change in size and of foreshortening. In order to work properly, the viewing point must be placed at any position other than head-on, and the objects should be assumed to be of relatively equal size. Because letterforms are so familiar to the viewer and the visual clues to the identity of each letterform so easily recognized, they make a perfect foil for this kind of perspective treatment.

One of the earliest examples of incorporating photography into typographic design is Laszlo Moholy-Nagy's poster for Pneumatik tires **(Fig. 1.5)**. Rather than using the tire as the image, the poster demonstrates its functional use through the typographic treatment. This photomontage was a prototype and never produced commercially. An innovator in the use of photography as a communication medium, Moholy-Nagy called this new method *fotoplastik* and *typofoto*, and it uses a combination of photographic process and hand illustration.

1.5 Lazlo Moholy-Nagy, *Pneumatik*, 1923. Collection, Museum of Modern Art, New York.

3

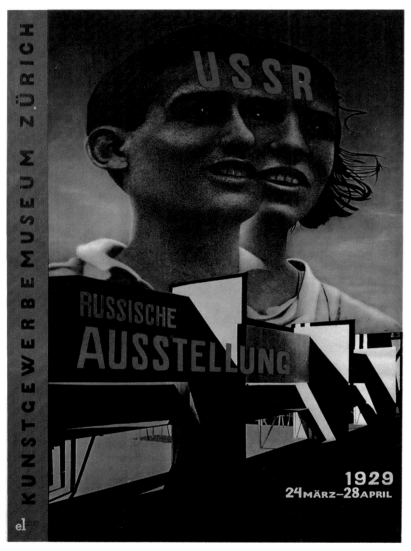

1.6 El Lissitzky, *USSR Russische Austellung* poster, 1929. From the collection of Merrill C. Berman, New York City.

Moholy-Nagy's work was one of the first to reveal that the combination of photographic process and typographic design enabled the letterform and word to become more expressive and dynamic. It also demonstrated that the typographic word could possess some of the same characteristics used by images, such as movement and occupation of space.

Moholy-Nagy's composition is visually complex in that the typography not only moves away from the viewer by converging, but it also angles and curves in space. The addition of the abstract hand-drawn "racetrack" lines and photographic image of the automobile enhance the typography's visual statement by combining the visual ideas of the race car, its implied speed and movement, and the racetrack.

Moholy-Nagy carefully controlled the compositional elements in order to achieve the most dramatic effects. The elements bleed—or extend beyond the top edge, sides, and bottom of the format—a technique that has a tendency to cause the poster to expand visually. The racetrack lines on which the type and race car rest converge and disappear into space and therefore increase compositional depth. The light, transparent, abstract roadway image in the foreground helps tie the elements together into a unified composition. Such compositional techniques are some of the fundamental visual forces that make this piece dynamic, and they are often used by other designers in other contexts to achieve visual expression.

A poster that demonstrates the dramatic impact and potential of photomontage and converging typography is El Lissitzky's *USSR Russische Austellung* poster **(Fig. 1.6)**. Lissitzky was an architect, painter, photographer, and graphic designer, and his multidisciplinary approach is readily recognized in the *USSR Russische Austellung* poster. The two youthful figures are merged into a single image via photomontage, and the USSR typography becomes part of that symbolic image. Lissitzky's interest in the illusion of three dimensions on a flat surface is revealed as the planes, shades, and shadows of the hand-drawn panels recede into space. The illusion of the panels moving back in space is intensified by the converging typography, "Russische Austellung," which rests on the same imaginary plane. This movement in space is further reinforced by the flat plane on which the dates rest and particularly by the bold red vertical rule. The composition is visually complex because of the many elements and changes in space and position. The de-

1.7 Max Huber, *Italstrade s/a* poster, 1941.

1.8 Max Huber, *Gran Premio dell' Autodromo Monza* poster, 1948.

signer composes, controls, and reduces these elements to their most powerful elemental visual terms.

In 1940 Max Huber began a career-long interest in the photographic manipulation of both words and images. His earliest work consists of experimental photograms that investigate light, movement, and the illusion of depth. By 1941 he had synthesized these ideas with both the typography and image of the Italstrade road construction poster **(Fig. 1.7)**. The use of converging perspective in both the typography and the stylized image of the mountain roadway contribute to the viewer's sense of depth, movement, and visual excitement.

The transparency of the typographic plane not only enables the viewer to experience fully the convoluted roadway but also ties together the typography and image. In 1948, Huber developed these visual themes further in the Monza poster **(Fig. 1.8)**. More technically complex, the Monza poster abstracts the imagery of the roadway racetrack into a series of arrowlike transparent planes, and the typography occupies still deeper space; all this is enhanced by the illusion of transparency, so that the elements seem to move and overlap in space. The transparency of the words and images enables them to work in concert as a unified visual statement.

In both the Huber and Moholy-Nagy posters, the convergence of the principal typography becomes a central image. Extending the elements beyond the edges expands the format visually, and the sense of infinite compositional space is heightened as the elements converge in deepest visual space. All the limited typography on the Monza poster converges to a single point, which helps maintain the visual order and increase the visual dynamics. The converged typography on the Italstrade poster is modified by the horizontal subordinate type in a grid structure that aligns with and relates to the other compositional elements. Both methods of working with the typography have their own merits, and the selection of the appropriate technique depends on the amount of copy and the visual complexity of the elements.

5

1.9 Greg Thomas, *Type As Texture* typographic experiments, 1972.

1.10 Greg Thomas, *Type in Space* typographic experiments, 1972.

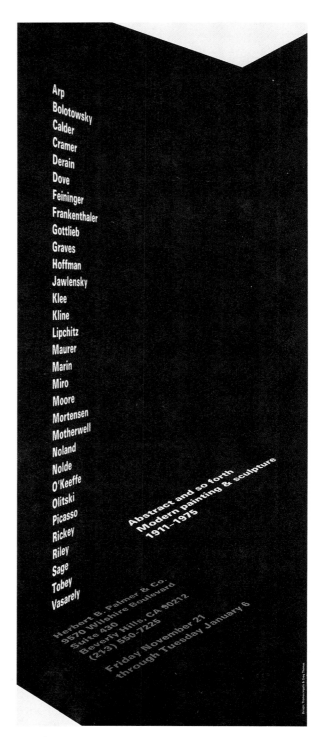

1.11 Greg Thomas, *Abstract and So Forth Modern Painting and Sculpture 1911–1975* poster, 1978.

Both the texture of typography and the movement of type in space were part of the personal visual experiments of Greg Thomas in the early 1970s **(Figs. 1.9, 1.10)**. The changes between foreground and background space and position that were created by combining typographic textures of varying intensity are seen in Thomas's *Type As Texture* experimental composition. The dynamic movement of textured planes released from a flat frontal existence in *Type in Space* opened up a new world of visual possibilities.

The viewer is invited into the abstract illusory space created in Thomas's *Abstract and So Forth...* poster **(Fig. 1.11)**. As the typography of the artist's names moves back in space, it creates a "wall" surface and converges toward a corner of the "room" that is suggested by the triangular white ceiling and floor areas at the top and bottom of the poster. The "floor" is further suggested by the name of the gallery and other relevant information. The invisible plane, on which the typography of the exhibition's title rests, floats somewhere above the floor. The typography is organized with a flush left edge that helps the viewer with visual organization and orientation. The flush left edge of the artists' names defines the wall plane, and the edges of the other two blocks of copy are parallel to the white edge of the "floor." A final beautiful detail is the cropping of the top white "ceiling" triangle on the right side, which is a subtle clue to the nature of the space that the poster format surrounds.

Yukihisa Takakita's forceful *CREATION* poster was made for an exhibition of his own work **(Fig. 1.12)**. The dynamic visual impact of the converged typography is heightened by the tensions created by the last letterform in the word CREATION, the *N*. The proximity of the top and bottom corners to the edge of the format creates a visual tension and emphasizes impact.

It is interesting that the word CREATION reads from background to foreground as all other examples of convergence shown here read from foreground to background. This may be explained by the fact that the designer is Japanese and therefore is less bound by the Western conventions of reading. Another possibility is that tensions created by the closeness of the sharp angled corners of the *N* to the edge of the poster could not be depicted with the same drama as the rounded form of the *C* suggests.

Despite the abstract, out-of-focus manner in which the first letters in CREATION appear, they still are legible, and the word is eminently readable. The perspective principle of the focus effect is also at work, whereby the

1.12 Yukihisa Takakita, *CREATION* exhibition poster, 1980.

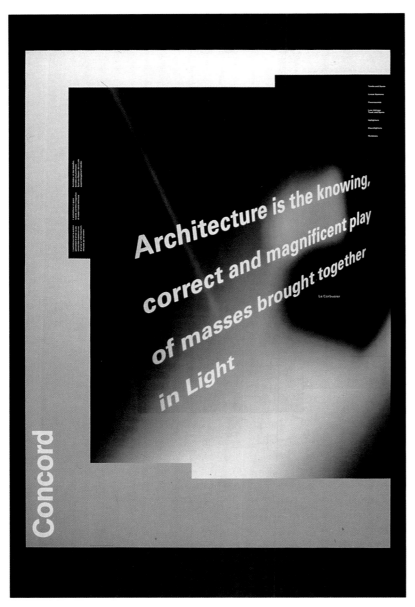

1.13 Eight Five Zero, Poster for Concord Lighting, 1986.

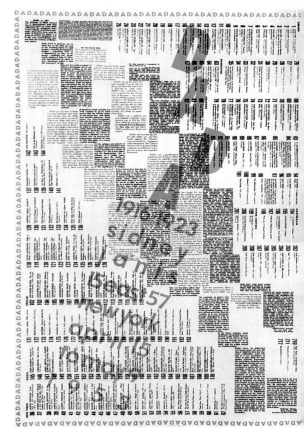

1.14 Marcel Duchamp and Sidney Janis, *DADA* poster, 1953. Collection, Museum of Modern Art, New York. Gift of the Sidney Janis Gallery. Copyright ARS N.Y./ADAGP, 1988.

letters closest to the viewer are sharp and in focus, and as they recede in space, they become more out of focus. By working with typographic convergence, the focus effect can also be reversed; that is, the letters close to the viewer can appear soft and out of focus, and those farther from the viewer can be sharp. This principle is based on the way in which the human eye focuses: The eye chooses either foreground or background as its prime area of focus, and the other areas then take on a blurry appearance. This method is thus consciously used by the designer to control the how the work will be viewed.

The shaped compositional window of the Eight Five Zero poster for Concord Lighting intensifies the converged typography and diffused light image **(Fig. 1.13)**. The viewer peers into a very deep, dark, mysterious space that surrounds the quotation, and as the type moves deeper in space, so too does the viewer's eye. The source for the quotation, Le Corbusier, is set in face-front, flat, very small typography that pulls the space of

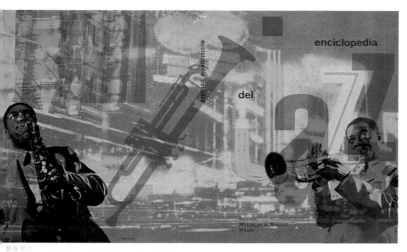

1.15 Max Huber, *Enciclopedia del Jazz* cover, 1952.

the composition even farther away. To add to the intriguing nature of this work, the deep-space image bleeds off the right side of the format, abruptly terminating the compositional depth.

Transparency and Overlapping

The illusion of transparency is dependent on a change in value and overlapping position. Within those compositions that use a full range of color, the tones can be subtle combinations of the two or more objects depicted. Black-and-white compositions may use tones of gray or textures and patterns to achieve similar results. Color compositions can create additional hues through mixtures of the colors that overlap. In both black-and-white and color compositions, the resulting color changes can greatly enhance the visual quality.

By using the principle of transparency, multiple planar surfaces are directly implied. Because these planes can appear to be incredibly thin, a change in size is not necessary for the illusion. Even when there is no change in the object's size or no additional perspective clues, the resulting change in tone can be dramatic. In many instances, transparency takes the place of the shade and shadow that would naturally occur in overlapping. It redirects the composition so that the viewer's eye travels through the elements. In dynamic compositions, it can also intensify the perception of movement.

The *DADA* poster by Marcel Duchamp and Sidney Janis represents an unusual form of transparency **(Fig. 1.14)**. This composition uses typography as the textural structure on which the foreground's large diagonal format letterforms rest. The background repetition of the blocks of small type in varying weights directs the viewer's eye from the top left to the bottom right. The opposing diagonal of the larger message creates a graphic *x*, appropriate to the Dada movement of the early twentieth century, which was against just about everything, including the functional role of typography. The Dadaists used typography as texture and form, which then created a nonfunctional visual sense of its own. In the background textures of this poster, the letterforms combine to create an abstract texture. They also convey information, as the background text is the catalog for the exhibition. Transparency in this case permits a dual message in a single composition.

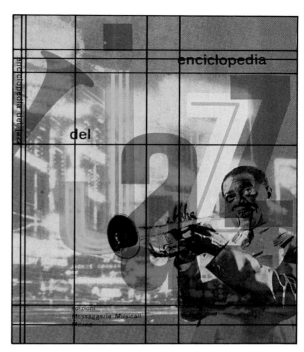

1.16 Max Huber, *Enciclopedia del Jazz* cover, visual structure.

In 1952 Max Huber experimented with the transparency of images and type in his cover for an encyclopedia of jazz **(Fig. 1.15)**. Using a scene of city nightlife as a base, he juxtaposed images of a trumpet player, a silhouette of a trumpet, overlapping transparent letterforms for the word *jazz*, and finally a top layer of black copy. This composition exudes a strong feeling of mood, depth, complexity, and excitement, similar to those emotions evoked by the music itself. The complexity of this composition shows the many visual problems in controlling so many layers and elements. This is similar to that of the Italstrade poster in which a horizontal/vertical grid composition is used on the top layer of type to help in visual control, and the alignment of the top layer of elements with those on lower layers assists in creating cohesive visual relationships **(Fig. 1.16)**.

The visual control of horizontal/vertical elements within an ordered and visually related grid system is an ideal method for the designer to retain control over the composition. The contrast of the carefully placed subordinate elements with the spontaneous-appearing transparent elements holds together the composition as a whole and organizes the manner in which the viewer perceives it. Because the color black was chosen for the control elements, they appear to advance toward the viewer and occupy the foreground top layer of space.

1.17 Bob Noorda, Pirelli Tires poster, 1959.

In 1959, Bob Noorda explored the role of typography as image in his work for the Pirelli Tire Company **(Fig. 1.17)**. The company logotype—sans serif bold expanded letterforms and an unusually expanded bowl of the uppercase *P*—plus radial overlapping transparency and movement were used to communicate the essence and motion of tires. Surrounded by the silhouette form of a tire, the message is unmistakable.

The logotype, Pirelli, not only identified the manufacturer but also became an image for the company's product, tires. This composition, though relatively simple in context and form, enabled the word to become a kinetic image appropriate to the task of communication. Obviously the compositional license taken with the cropping of this piece could not have been successful if the logotype were less well known or familiar to the viewer. But because of great visual familiarity with the logotype over a long period of time this kind of typographic manipulation is indeed possible.

Modern Planar Typography

A sophisticated relationship between color and transparency exists in the poster for a publisher and bookstore by Kurt Wirth **(Fig. 1.18)**. Each color appears to be resting on its own plane and the resulting implied depth contributes to the composition's lyrical qualities. As the colors overlap, additional color mixtures are created, resulting in very beautiful subcompositions within the composition. The transparency of the printing inks helps make this poster rich and vibrant, as all of the colors are printed at 100 percent of their value.

The transparency of the color is enhanced by the placement of the letters near the top of the compositional format. This top placement is associated with the relational element of gravity, a visual psychological perception, that "heavier" (usually darker in color and more compact in form) elements will rest at the bottom of the page and "lighter" (usually lighter in color and more expansive in form) elements will rise to the top.

Because of the layering effects that can be achieved by overlapping elements, depth cues can be generated and compositions can become alive through the use of contrast and illusions of movement and depth. Two words seem to move together and to begin to merge as

10

1.18 Kurt Wirth, bookstore promotional poster, 1974.

1.19 Kimberly Elam, *Film & Video* detail from a brochure for the Ohio Arts Council, 1987.

one in the *Film & Video* brochure (**Fig. 1.19**). The contrast between the two words is heightened by the use of a serif typeface and a sans serif condensed typeface, and as both the words and the type styles blend, the differences are underscored.

Depth and movement on a two-dimensional surface attract the eye because the viewer knows that even though a flat static surface exists, his or her perceptions have been tricked into seeing the animation of movement or the space and distance associated with depth. Overlapping elements not only can create the appearance of a change in planes but also can indicate transparency, by producing additional tones.

1.20 Rolf Muller, *Kieler Woche 1972* poster, 1972.

Curving and Bending Planes

As with movement, the curving and bending of planes in space are implied by distorting the surface plane on which the typography rests. Typographic characters are excellent subjects for the visual communication of curving and bending, as the eye is programmed to see letterforms in a single-plane, horizontal, frontal context. The slightest distortion of the letterform by curving, bending, or twisting the surface plane is immediately noticed, and the eye is fascinated by letterforms that leave this frontal position for a change in point of view.

An awareness of the invisible plane on which all typography rests is important to understanding the effect of implied movement. For the designer, the recognition of such a plane and the acknowledgment of an infinite compositional window with the potential for limitless space are essential to both understanding and developing such compositions.

Curving and bending in typography are closely linked with the other perspective principles of convergence, transparency, and movement. As in convergence, letters diminish in space as they recede from the viewer, although in a much less regular fashion than in perspective convergence. The invisible surface plane strongly implies its shape in the distortion of the letterforms. Occasionally, this surface plane can act in the same way as does the principle of closure; that is, as an invisible object. For example, note the implied sail in Rolf Muller's *Kieler Woche 1972* poster **(Fig. 1.20)**. In many such compositions, the visual effect of implied movement is created by the flowing convoluted structure of the surface plane.

Rolf Muller's *Kieler Woche 1972* poster, which advertises sailing races, is stunning in its visual simplicity and communication of form. The curving and bending of the surface plane represents the type as if it were a sail billowing in the wind. Consisting of just a few words and the dates of the event, the poster has an appealing visual directness. The typography acts not only as specific verbal information but also as a connotative visual image, as the surface plane on which the typography rests is interpreted as a sail.

The blue background of this poster has connotations of sky or water, both appropriate to the subject of sailing races. The soft gray color of the typography, *Kieler*

1.A Kimberly Elam, instructor, Lisa Weber, designer,
Typographic composition *Calder*, The Ohio State University,
Department of Industrial Design, 1985.

1.B Kimberly Elam, instructor, Kathy Shaw, designer,
Typographic composition *Calder*, The Ohio State University,
Department of Industrial Design, 1985.

Challenged to try their hand at planar typography and
perspective, advanced typography students at the Ohio
State University, Department of Industrial Design, created the two compositions in **Figures 1.A and 1.B**. They
are based on the work of the sculptor Alexander Calder
and accordingly use the word *Calder* as the principal
visual element. Focusing on Calder's kinetic mobiles,
the compositions' form and color are notable for their
visual reference. As the discussion and work pro-
gressed, interest in the possibilities of multiple-plane
compositions intensified. In these two examples, the
designers chose to break the image out of the square
compositional format in order to sharpen the implied
space and dimension. The letterforms are constructed
by hand, and each one occupies its own plane in space
and converges to its own point in space. Deep background
colors were found to increase the perception of space.
Admittedly, the readability of the word *Calder* is reduced
by this visual treatment. However, the resulting compositions are rich in connotative meaning and become
images themselves.

In the *Zen* and *Kodak* experimental student compositions, polycontrast print
paper was used as a medium to explore the transparency principle **(Figs. 1.C,
1.D)**. A black-and-white print process was chosen because it is highly plastic
and offers a rich vocabulary to the typographic designer. In addition to a bright
white and dense black, most polycontrast print papers are capable of
producing seven or more distinct gray tones and gradations of unlimited
range, which invite experimentation. These effects, from the most subtle
differentiations of gray to the most dramatic black and white contrast, are
readily controlled and present visual possibilities impossible to achieve as
easily with any other means.

Two methods are useful for experimenting with typography as it curves or
bends in space. The first method is to compose the typography on clear plastic
or thin malleable paper and to distort physically the plastic or paper **(Fig. 1.E)**.
The second method is to use the hand graphic technique of a distorted grid
on which to project the letterform **(Fig. 1.F)**. Both techniques work well, with
the paper or plastic distortion technique having the advantage of rapid
spontaneous exploration, and the distortion grid technique having the advantage of ultimate control of the process.

1.21 George Tscherny, *José de Rivera* exhibition catalog cover, 1961.

Woche 1972, increases the flowing movement of the letterforms. In direct contrast with their size, form, and color, the dates, 4.bis 11.Juni, which appear in green, offer a visual strength and a stabilizing influence.

Experiments by George Tscherny in 1961 revealed the camera's dramatic potential for distorting typography **(Fig. 1.21)**. By bending and curving letterforms under the camera, a unique image was created for the sculptor José de Rivera, whose work uses bent surfaces. The image shown here is the front cover, spine, and back cover for an exhibition catalog of Rivera's work. Resisting the obvious solutions to a project of this kind, Tscherny used the typography to develop an exciting identity of the image, which accordingly contributed to the viewers' understanding of the artist's work.

It is clear that Tscherny carefully controlled the movement and distortion of the letterforms in order to maintain readability; yet at the same time he allowed the typographic image to create a sense of depth, space, and movement. The dimensional form and format, front cover, spine, and back cover of the book is acknowledged by the manner in which the typography moves across the covers and is cropped when the book is closed. In addition, the front cover has been carefully designed to reveal the last name of the artist, Rivera.

A complex and compelling visual image was created by Steff Geissbuhler on a brochure cover for Geigy **(Fig. 1.22)**. The type seems to spiral down a deep, cavernous tunnel into infinity. As the type moves in the composition, so does the viewer's eye, which perceives a limitless visual space. In this composition

1.22 Steff Geisbuhler, Geigy brochure cover, 1965.

13

Swimaster

1.24 Eugene Grossman, AMF Swimaster Fins package typography, 1978.

1.23 Siegfried Odermatt, *Wasser* brochure, 1968.

the legibility of the type is diminished by this treatment in favor of the visual excitement created by the movement and distortion. Geissbuhler controlled the distortion in order to permit enough visual cues to allow the viewer to read the word *Geigy*.

Geissbuhler's work, in particular, takes advantage of the far-reaching compositional window. The composition bleeds off all four sides of the page, visually expanding the format. The radial movement of the typography directs the viewer's attention to the center of the format, and the black background has unmistakable connotations of space or water.

Siegfried Odermatt used the natural effect of water as a magnifier in his brochure cover **(Fig. 1.23)**. The illusion of water, an invisible fluid, is created and reinforced by the bubbles at the top of the water surface. The typography below the surface of the water is affected by magnification and a slight degree of distortion. The distorted portion of the typography is enhanced by its direct contrast with the set type above the waterline. This treatment also has aural implications, in that the emphasis in pronunciation is placed on the latter half of the word.

Manipulated typography can be used not only for posters, but also for all other forms of visual communication, including packaging. The Swimaster typography was designed by Eugene Grossman for a package for swimmer's fins, and it is an example of how the word as image can become the image of the product **(Fig. 1.24)**. The curving and bending of the word *Swimaster* instantly produces the images of water, swimming, waves, and motion, thereby precluding the necessity for photographic or illustrative images of the product or of the acquatic environment in which the product is used. Portions of the letters are hidden from view as the surface plane of the typography bends "in the water." But again, the letters' legibility is not affected, as enough visual clues to letterforms' identities remain.

Charles Eames pioneered the technology of bending plywood for industrial applications and, most notably, for use in manufacturing of furniture of his own design. In Gordon Salchow's *Eames* poster, the curvilinear

1.25 Gordon Salchow, *Eames* poster, 1978.

typography is reminiscent of Eames's bent plywood furniture and also provides a strong visual contrast with the highly structured images and typography **(Fig. 1.25)**. Close-up details of the beautiful forms of Eames's furniture are highlighted in a crisply cropped format that gives the poster a sense of visual structure. The typography curves, bends, and recedes in space, an effect that is enhanced by bleeding it off the edge. The block of copy on the left of the poster has a shaped, curved edge that mirrors the curves of the photographs. The communication of the message is also sharpened by the visual structure and contrasts of form.

The desert sand forms a ground for Greg Thomas's *Seven Artists in Israel* poster **(Fig. 1.26)**. The typography undulates as if projected onto or written in the sand-and-rock background. In addition to the typography's fluid movement, the composition is carefully ordered and controlled to strengthen its communication. Within the hierarchy of typographic information, the title of the exhibition is brought out in black as being the most important or first level of communication. The artists' names appear in white, which reflects the brightness of the light on the textured ground and gives them a second level of importance. Finally, specific information regarding the place and dates of the exhibition are reversed out of black at the bottom as the third level. The flush left edge of the type aligns with the rock in the textured background, and the smaller rock edge follows the rag of the type to create a relationship between the typography and the ground.

1.26 Greg Thomas, *Seven Artists in Israel* poster for the Los Angeles County Museum of Art, 1978.

15

1.27 Marcel Duchamp, *Nude Descending a Staircase No. 2*, 1912. Oil on canvas, 58" x 35". Philadelphia Museum of Art, Louise and Walter Arensberg Collection.

1.28 Giacomo Balla, *Dynamism of a Dog on a Leash*, 1912. Oil on canvas, 35⅝" x 43¼". Albright-Knox Art Gallery, Buffalo, N.Y. Bequest of A. Conger Goodyear and Gift of George F. Goodyear, 1964.

Movement

Few techniques can make typography as animated as the illusion of motion or movement. The popularization of photography and experiments with sequential photography by Eadweard Muybridge in the late nineteenth century interested painters of the cubist and futurist movements. Marcel Duchamp experimented with motion studies by repeating abstracted planes in his painting *Nude Descending a Staircase* (**Fig. 1.27**). Futurist Giacomo Balla was also intrigued with motion created by repetition in his painting *Dynamism of a Dog on a Leash* (**Fig. 1.28**). The conceptual intent of Duchamp and Balla was to capture motion on the static surface of a painting.

Modern materials and technology have developed new methods of implying movement. Light-sensitive photographic paper will reveal a "light trail" if a film negative is moved across it while it is exposed to light. The resulting image is similar to the exhaust trail left by a jet airplane. The viewer's eye perceives an unmistakable movement of form and, in some instances, an aural sensation of whooshing movement. The movement of repeated elements can be enhanced by the illusion of transparency that is created by overlapping transparent inks or halftone screens. The repeated elements move in a linear manner and also create the illusion of depth as the viewer perceives multiple planes that light passes through.

Bob Noorda's Pirelli poster uses a similar cropping technique to intensify the feeling of movement (**Fig. 1.29**). In the *Pirelli Più Veloce* poster the letterforms are redrawn in order to conform to a circular pathway without

1.29 Bob Noorda, *Più Veloce* Pirelli Tires poster, 1959.

1.30 Inge Druckrey, Orta Softdrinks poster, 1966.

jagged edges, which might inhibit the perception of swift movement. Darker, broader portions of the letterforms create darker shapes while being moved during exposure. The gray trail fades into space, and the cropping of the letterform image strengthens its dynamic quality. Circular compositional forces are the most visually compelling and have meanings associated with encompassment, repetition, and warmth.[1]

Inge Druckrey used repetition, transparency, and color change to create movement in her Orta softdrinks poster **(Fig. 1.30)**. The company name, Orta, is repeated as a solid form and also as a line screen, with the width of the lines and color as variable elements. Similar to the carbon dioxide bubbles in sparkling sodas, the typography moves and undulates in a moving pattern. The horizontal/vertical grid structure of this poster is emphasized by the seemingly random color and texture changes of the word *Orta*. Restraint and sensitivity are used in the placement of the typography on a white field that softens the colors.

---

1. Dondis A. Dondis, *A Primer of Visual Literacy*, Cambridge: MIT Press, 1973, p. 46.

Fred Troller's poster for American Airlines is very simple and consists of only three words and an implied image **(Fig. 1.31)**. However, the animation of the word *Boston* is clearly indicative of the speed and movement of air travel. The diagonal movement of the type creates a composition that is intensely provoking, and by cropping the piece on both the top and left edges, it further intensifies the visual feeling of movement. The baseline of the word *Boston* is perpendicular to the baselines of the words *American Airlines*. This is a extreme contrast of direction that emphasizes the movement of the word *Boston*. Diagonal composition is the most unsettling of the three movement directions and offers the designer a dynamic tool with which to communicate.

The slightly later Arizona poster uses movement in another direction with different connotative meaning **(Fig. 1.32)**. The word *Arizona* rises vertically from the bottom of the poster in a manner reminiscent of desert heat. This feeling is further intensified by the rich, warm, golden colors of the sunset.

These works were probably produced by dragging a negative film across print paper while it was exposed to light. This creates a light trail or, more accurately, a graytone trail that has strong connotations of motion. This movement illusion can be manipulated and intensified further by extending the image beyond the format boundaries. "Motion" trails that bleed off the edge of the compositional frame imply that the space of the composition is not limited to the paper surface but also embraces the space surrounding the composition and thus expands the compositional area in the viewer's perception. The eye moves off the page in order to seek the source of the image but keeps returning to the composition. This illusion of movement creates visual energy that can be intensified by contrasting the static and active elements.

The series of experimental covers by Helmut Schmid explores the possibilities of texture and the movement of type on the page **(Figs. 1.33** through **1.35)**. Each cover was made using metal type and hand-set characters. While being printed, the typeset block is moved after each impression on the letterpress, and the same sheet of paper is repeatedly sent through the press. The rhythmic movement of the type and the frequent repetition reduce the words to a texture, and only on careful examination can they be read. Helmut Schmid described the process in his book, *Typography Today*:

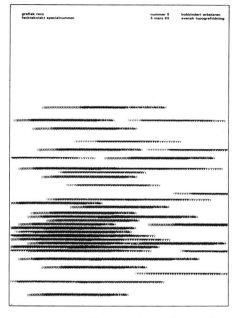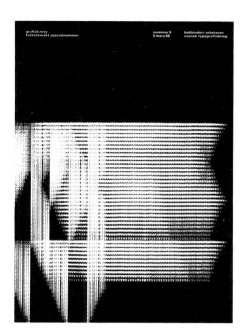

1.33, 1.34, 1.35 Helmut Schmid, *Grafisk Revy* magazine cover series, 1964.

"The results are controlled accidents with rhythmic points, with shorter and longer lines, with open and congested areas, with readable and unreadable type, with stasis and movement."[2] Each direction has its own visual response: Horizontal/vertical compositions have a sense of orderliness and solidity; diagonal compositions are visually exciting and dynamic; and circular compositions command strong visual attention and are psychologically reassuring.[3]

As with many of the other principles and techniques discussed in this chapter, the addition of color to this technique opens new visual variables as the effects of transparency and overlapping come into play.

2. Helmut Schmid, *Typography Today*, Tokyo: Seibundo Shinkosha, 1980, p. 96.
3. Dondis A. Dondis, *A Primer of Visual Literacy*, Cambridge: MIT Press, 1973, p. 46.

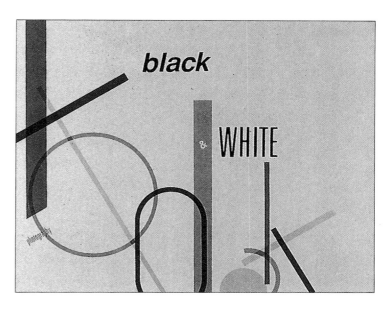

1.C Kimberly Elam and P. Lyn Middleton, instructors, Amy Coiner, designer, *Zen* composition, North Carolina State University, Department of Product and Visual Design, 1988.

1.D Kimberly Elam, instructor, Jerry Durkin, designer, *Kodak* composition, The Ohio State University, Department of Industrial Design, 1988.

1.E (series of 2) Kimberly Elam, instructor, student designer, *Typography* curving and bending compositions, The Ohio State University, Department of Industrial Design, 1987.

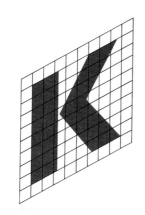

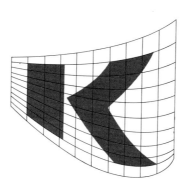

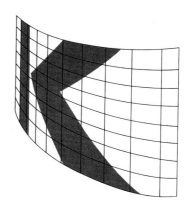

1.F (series of 4) Kimberly Elam, instructor, student designer, Hand-manipulated grid *K*, The Ohio State University, Department of Industrial Design, 1984.

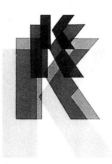

1.G (series of 2) Kimberly Elam, instructor, student designer, Movement *k*, The Ohio State University, Department of Industrial Design.

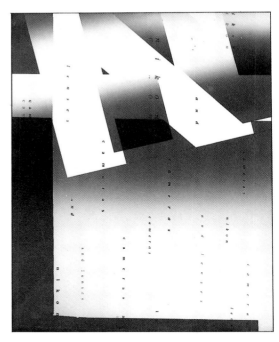

1.H Kimberly Elam, instructor, Lois Jensen, designer, *Nikon* composition, North Carolina State University, Department of Product and Visual Design, 1988.

The black-and-white print process was the medium for students' experiments with the visual illusion of motion **(Figs. 1.G** through **1.I)**. Photography was again chosen, as it is by nature a medium of illusion. It freezes instants of time, space, and image. Black-and-white photography possesses surreal qualities, owing to the absence of a range of color; that is, everything is reduced to a nether world of black, white, and gray. The absence of color causes the eye to search for subtle nuances of tone, texture, space, shadow, and position. This lack of color distraction accordingly enables the viewer to investigate more closely and to perceive minute differences of tone, which become the visual clues of depth.

A method of animating typography is to repeat elements. With this method the principle of transparency comes into play, as in the animated *k* samples. The gray tones created by the step-and-repeat exposure gives the composition additional depth, and the change in position offers a sense of sequence. The method used here involves hand-cut masks, or kodaliths, that are moved over the print paper during exposure to produce a variety of special effects. Smooth and continuous movements by hand during exposure produce a light trail of gray tones that have strong connotations of movement and motion. This light trail can be controlled by the time of the exposure and the speed with which the negative is moved across the photographic print paper.

The *Viewpoints* and *Light and Typography* compositions are experimental work from an advanced typography course taught by Bill Deere. Each student was asked to create a project investigating type in a way that they had never used before.

The *Viewpoints* compositions used three-dimensional letterforms spelling the word, *viewpoints*, which were photographed in different environments, from different viewpoints, and with different light sources **(Fig. 1.J)**. The results are dramatically different in each work. The

1.I Kimberly Elam, instructor, Elaine Selden, designer, *Nikon* composition, North Carolina State University, Department of Product and Visual Design, 1988.

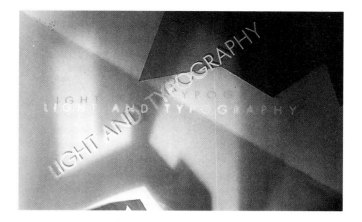

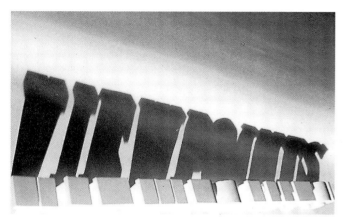

1.K (series of 2) Bill Deere, instructor, Sheila Nichols, designer, *Light and Typography,* experimental typography and photography composition, North Carolina State University, Department of Product and Visual Design, 1988.

1.J (series of 3) Bill Deere, instructor, Teddi Brown, designer, *Viewpoints,* experimental typography and photography composition, North Carolina State University, Department of Product and Visual Design, 1988.

first composition places the letterforms on a sheet of glass and photographs the typography from below. The second composition photographs the typography through a glass, with the type revealed only as a shadow on a draped background. The third composition photographs the type and shadow as reflected in a mirror.

The *Light and Typography* composition investigates the effects of shadowing and layering typography **(Fig. 1.K)**. The typography was manipulated by two means: First, it was placed on a pane of glass above a textured background; and second, a slide of the typography was placed in a projector and projected onto the background surface. Different effects were achieved by altering the distance of the glass from the background, moving the position of the projected type, and shifting the light source. These experiments demonstrate that typography has many possibilities beyond the usual two-dimensional surface.

2.1 Pisani, Genoa, 1640. *Masterpieces of Calligraphy*, Peter Jensen, editor, 1959, Dover.

2.2 Snell, London, 1723. *Masterpieces of Calligraphy*, Peter Jensen, editor, 1959, Dover.

2.3 Bourgoin, Paris, ca. 1810. *Masterpieces of Calligraphy*, Peter Jensen, editor, 1959, Dover.

Chapter 2
Handwritten Typography

Handwritten Typography

Handwriting is a form of drawing based on the linear strokes and marks that can be made by the hand. These strokes and marks are organized in a common system of construction that forms the individual visual signs of the alphabet, which, in sequence, become words.

In a literate society, handwriting implies no specialized skills beyond legibility, no particular aesthetic quality, and no specialized tools. Handwriting is commonplace in our everyday lives and yet is rare in visual messages. Indeed, it is so common that it is often overlooked as a form of typography and is rightly considered much less formal, legible, and precise than is set typography. When used to communicate messages, it is chosen because it offers so much more than specific information, as handwritten messages become dymanic statements of individual style, personal communication, and spontaneous creation and placement.

The Historical Context: Western Calligraphic Tradition

Western culture developed a rich tradition of calligraphy throughout the medieval period, from the fifth century until the fifteenth century. Although this period is also known as the Dark Ages, a shining light at this time was the illuminated manuscript tradition, which flourished in monasteries as a means of preserving and circulating religious texts. Parallels can also be drawn between the emphasis on medieval cathedral architecture and the illuminated manuscript. The design and layout of the manuscript page are based on architectonic principles of proportion, similar to those of the cathedral. The decorative elements of the initial letters are similar in purpose to those of the stained glass windows, as embellishment of the text with illustrations became a means of education, decoration, and enhancement of meaning. Just as the light that filtered through the stained glass window hinted at mysticism and allegory, so too did the illuminated manuscript, on which light was reflected from gold or silver leaf and in rich colors.

The decline of the illuminated manuscript tradition can be directly attributed to the invention and rapid popularization of the printing press. In about 1450, Johann Gutenberg brought together the technology and technique of printing, which changed the world forever. During a remarkable period of change known as the *incunabla* (cradle), from 1450 to 1500, over 35,000 editions and 9 million books were printed, markedly increasing the quantity and distribution of available information. In addition to books, pamphlets, religious treatises, and broadsides were printed, all predecessors of the poster and newspaper.

The invention of printing did not, however, suppress the calligraphic tradition, but rather initiated a more expanded use of handwriting with the extension of knowledge and learning (**Figs. 2.1** through **2.3**). Writing styles were developed that were more fluid, natural, and efficient for a variety of hands and skill levels. A good scriptwriting hand was considered the mark of an educated, cultured, and refined individual. And legible script was indispensable to the communication of information and the development of trade. Law and government officers frequently employed scribes or clerks to write and copy contracts, laws, and other agreements.

Copybooks that demonstrated the correct form for handwriting were first produced from engraved wood

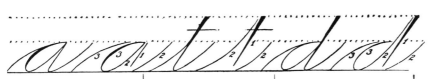

The letter A consists of upward left curve, downward left curve, upward right curve, downward straight line, upward right curve.
Analysis: Principles 3, 3, 2, 1, 2.

The letter T consists of upward left curve, downward straight line, upward right curve, horizontal straight line, one and a half spaces from base line.
Analysis: Principles 2, 1, 2.

The letter D consists of upward left curve, downward left curve, upward right curve, downward straight line, upward right curve.
Analysis Principles 3, 3, 2, 1, 2.

2.4 Script handwriting instructions, ca. nineteenth century. *Handbook of Early Advertising Art, Typographical Volume*, Clarence P. Hornung, 1947, Dover.

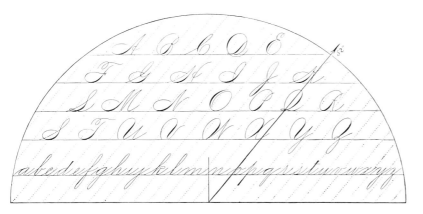

2.5 Script handwriting instructions, ca. nineteenth century. *Handbook of Early Advertising Art, Typographical Volume*, Clarence P. Hornung, 1947, Dover.

blocks, but by the late sixteenth century the fragile and soft wood blocks were replaced by metal plates **(Figs. 2.4, 2.5)**. The term *copperplate* describes a broad variety of scripts and is derived from the practice of engraving metal plates. Copperplate writing was produced by engraving letters into a metal plate with a sharp stylus. The deeper the scratch in the plate, the broader the stroke of the letter. The most efficient way to produce a copperplate engraving was to draw the word without lifting the stylus from the surface. The italic hand readily lent itself to this form of writing and resulted in the development of a more fluid script.

The first typefaces used in printing were designed to imitate as closely as possible the hand-drawn letterforms in calligraphic manuscripts. These bold characters were not uniform in manufacture; they lacked the contrast of thicks and thins and were very difficult to read. Throughout the centuries after printing was introduced, typefaces were gradually developed that had better proportion, consistent form, consistent measure, and greater legibility. As these typefaces were evolving, so too were the style and practice of handwriting. By the seventeenth century, printed type styles and handwritten type styles had become distinct, as had the attitudes toward their appropriate uses.

During the Industrial Revolution of the eighteenth and nineteenth centuries, society changed as people left the countryside for city factory work. A rapidly growing literate middle class with increased buying power stimulated the economy, and improvements in production and technology in the factories provided affordable merchandise. Machine made meant better made. A love of industry and the resulting prosperity for the working class were accompanied by a greater availability of books, literacy, and education, in combination with a multitude of goods and laborsaving devices.

The Industrial Revolution's perceptions of machine made as better made are still a part of our society. Modern culture is even more mechanized and continues to evolve along that path with the integration of the computer into society. The sense of craft and uniqueness has, for the most part, disappeared from everyday life. The role of the individual as creator, artist, and craftsperson has also largely disappeared. The calligraphic tradition of our predecessors is mostly forgotten. It is because of this decline in individual style that drawn letterforms are so appealing and seem to become even more so with the passage of time. Drawn letterforms reveal the hand of the creator and the existence of an individual designer.

Lithography and Illustrated Letterforms

Unwilling to settle for the available typefaces of the late nineteenth century and the restraints of letterpress printing, William Blake engraved, printed, and hand colored books of his own design, often books of his own poetry **(Fig. 2.6)**. The process of etching, which he had apprenticed and studied, permitted the creative freedom he required in illustrating typography and images. His books were printed in one color from etching plates, then colored individually by hand, and finally bound. The handcraft process limited the quantity of books Blake could produce but ensured their quality and free-flowing artistic expression. Blake's *Songs of Innocence*, a songbook for children published in 1789, demonstrates a style very different from that of most books of the time in that the typography is both illustrated and interconnected with the image. The resulting composition foreshadows art nouveau and the creative freedom later permitted by the chromolithographic process.

By the late eighteenth century most typography was printed by wood or metal type styles produced in factories and provided by the printer. Altering typography from what was available was a laborious and costly process and rarely was attempted. In contrast, handwriting consisted of defined methods of drawing letterforms in a legible manner and was reserved for law, business, and personal communication. The two forms of communicating with the written word could not be more different in attitude or aesthetics.

Near the end of the nineteenth century, the printing process of chromolithography began to offer artists, designers, and printers the challenge and opportunity to illustrate typography as part of a compositional whole. This printing process became prevalent and popular for its rich vivid colors and meticulous detail. Based on the simple principle that oil and water do not mix, smooth lithographic stones were marked with a wax crayon or pencil, moistened, and then inked, with the ink adhering only to the wax image. Paper was then laid on top of the inked image and the ink was transferred to the paper.

The lithographic process of printing requires that both type and image be drawn on a smooth stone surface for reproduction. Further, the letters had to be drawn in a reverse image on the stones so that they would be right-reading when printed. Although the letterforms often were traced, the resulting typography appeared less mechanical, and alterations and inventions in the letterforms were often made to suit the aesthetic sensibilities of the artist and/or the needs of the composition. Fre-

2.6 William Blake, *Songs of Innocence* title page, 1789. Library of Congress, Washington, D.C., Rosenwald Collection.

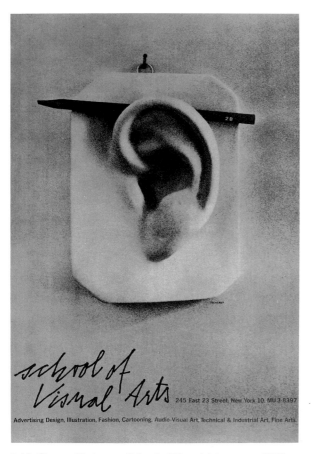

2.16 George Tscherny, *School of Visual Arts* poster, 1959.

2.17 Reudi Kulling, *Bic* poster, 1965.

Tscherny's innovative poster for the School of Visual Arts broke new ground with its combination of a photographed image and handwritten typography **(Fig. 2.16)**. Again, the visual connection of the pencil in the image to the handwriting on the poster, as well as to the programs at the school, is intensified by the typography. The viewer's eye is guided to the nail on the wall that has been pounded in by a hand, to the ear that was sculpted by hands, and to the pencil that assisted the hand in writing the typography on the poster. The visual logic is complete.

2.7 Arthur W. Dow, *Modern Art* poster, 1895. Library of Congress, Washington, D.C., Poster Collection.

quently, letterforms were drawn with the same flair as was the illustrated image. Released from the rigid horizontal/vertical lockup system of letterpress reproduction, the typography could now be placed on curves, run around the image, overlapped, and printed in a variety of vibrant colors.

The lithographic printing process was a prime influence in the art nouveau movement which flourished from about 1890 to 1910. The organic, fluid shapes of the art nouveau movement coupled beautifully with the improved technology accompanying chromolithography, as artists were not limited to the letterforms supplied by the printers.

A very early example of hand-drawn type styles can be seen in Arthur Dow's *Modern Art* poster with its painterly quality, imagery, and composition **(Fig. 2.7)**. The lithographic process extends and enhances the manner in which the typography is worked. Just as the floral vines in the background flow through the composition, so too does the typography. Obviously unbound by strict letterpress requirements, the baseline of the typography is as fluid and curvilinear as the composition is. The letterforms are soft, hand-painted shapes created with a brush and similar in style to the imagery. The variations in their size cause a shifting flow in the perception of space foreground to background, just as the visual space of the composition is a composition within a composition.

Pierre Bonnard and Jacques Villon were two of the many designers of the art nouveau period who illustrated the typography accompanying the illustrated image. In *France-Champagne* and *Le Grillon*, the same fluid lines of the images also appear in the typography **(Figs. 2.8 and 2.9)**. In *Le Grillion* the typography is drawn and composed with the same care and creativity as the

2.8 Pierre Bonnard, *France-Champagne*, 1891. Lithograph, 30$^{1}/_{8}$" x 23". Collection, Museum of Modern Art, New York, Purchase Fund.

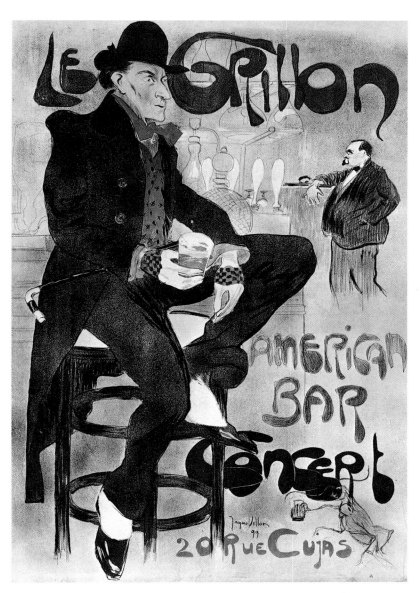

2.9 Jacques Villon, *Le Grillon* poster, 1899. Lithograph, 49" x 34$^{5}/_{8}$". Collection, Museum of Modern Art, New York, Purchase Fund.

image is. The flowing thicks and thins of the letterforms are similar to those in the images; and just as the images occupy foreground to background space, so too does the typography. The letterforms do not attempt to mimic the existing type styles of the time but are an extension of the illustrated image in every way.

In *France-Champagne*, the typography dances and bubbles as an extension of the image. It is impossible in letterpress typography to "kern"—reduce the space between letters—so tightly, to use such a range and combination of sizes, and to have such a curvilinear baseline. The typography both reflects and is a part of the joyful spirit of the image and the product. Bonnard and Villon, as well as many others of the art nouveau period, combined words and images in a single unified compositional style of fluid harmony. Because of the experimental abstraction and stylization of both type and image, this movement is recognized as one of the first phases of the modern art movement.

2.10 Oskar Kokoschka, *1908 Kunstschau* poster (woman cotton-picker), 1908. From the collection of Merrill C. Berman, New York City.

The developing modern styles in the fine arts in the early twentieth century are reflected in the images and typography of Oskar Kokoschka's *1908 Kunstschau* poster **(Fig. 2.10)**. Particularly in this poster can be seen the flat sense of space used by the Vienna secession movement, a quality that anticipated art deco and cubism. This work was produced while Kokoschka was a student at the Vienna School of Applied Arts and was also an associate of the Wiener Werkstätte, a modernist design workshop directed by the architect Josef Hoffmann. The typography is of the same style and texture as the image, both words and images being created by the same hand on the lithographic stone. Kokoschka isolated the typography at the top and bottom of the composition but formed the letters with the same black blunt strokes as the image so that they become a part of the composition.

Even though it was produced in 1920, Schnackenberg's *Odeon Casino* poster was strongly influenced by art nouveau **(Fig. 2.11)**. This is one of the few works of its time that used the expressionistic style of art nouveau even as design and typography were changing dramatically to more abstracted imagery and machine-set typography. Both the images and the typography are expressionistic in style, and the black tuxedo of the male dancer disappears into the black background in a manner similar to that of the Beggarstaffs design at the turn of the century. The separation of the typography from the image definitely does not show art nouveau influence but does foreshadow later work in which the separation of the type and image became the norm. The typography is in a cursive italic handwriting style whose slant echoes the movement of the dancers.

The expressionist typography of Lyonel Feininger's *Europaische graphick* title page is an anomaly in the work from the Bauhaus of the 1920s **(Fig. 2.12)**. Feininger, who was about fifty years old when he created this work, was one of the older teaching masters at the Bauhaus. During the pre-Bauhaus period he was trained and strongly influenced by medieval romanticism and the arts and crafts movement from which the Bauhaus evolved. This influence is revealed in the hand-carved and stylized letterforms. The influence of the developing Bauhaus attitude at the time of typographic functionalism is felt in the composition in the lack of a pictorial image.

Initially, the Bauhaus sought to develop a new unity of art and technology through knowledge of the arts of the past, expressionism, and crafts. This goal evolved radically into one that embraced the technological age and sought an objective visual language that would subjugate stylistic concerns and individual expression. By 1923 the evolution was complete, and Walter Gropius, one of the founders of the Bauhaus, changed the

2.11 Walter Schnackenberg, *Odeon Casino* poster, 1920.
From the collection of Merrill C. Berman, New York City.

school motto from "A Unity of Art and Handicraft" to "Art and Technology, a New Unity." The resulting influence on typography was the design of new rational sans serif type styles and a strong emphasis on the design of visual materials using technology and visual organizational principles.

The overwhelming Bauhaus influence on typography and the removal of the visible human hand from the style of letterforms prevailed, and visual emphasis shifted from expressionistic typographic design to the organization of cold, rational typography with nonobjective imagery. This goal is still a powerful and important part of the visual language of graphic design. Ironically, however, the developing technology that initiated this objective is now becoming one of the reasons for visual investigations into handcraft calligraphy, handwriting, and illustration. Because the evolving computer age has ordered, organized, and constructed almost all of what we see and hear, the cold visual language of rational typography has left us empty and yearning for a visual connection to the artist or designer. Handcraft in typography is such a visual connection from the designer to the viewer: It is a statement of individuality, humanity, and style, as it reveals thought, creative process, and human frailty through imperfection.

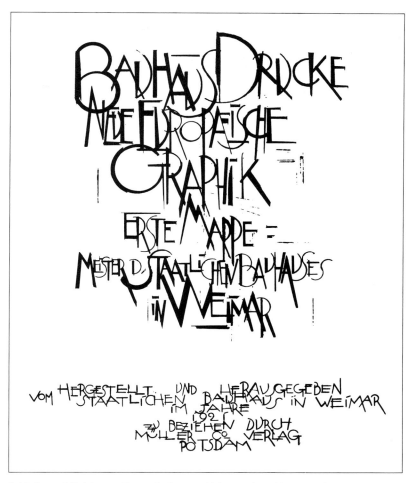

2.12 Lyonel Feininger, *Europaische graphick,* woodcut title page, 1921.
Photograph courtesy of the Museum of Modern Art, New York.
Copyright © 1988, by Cosmopress, Geneva.

2.13 Pablo Picasso, *Les Menines*, Galerie Louise Leiris, 1959.
Lithograph, 26³/₈" x 18³/₄". Collection, Museum of Modern Art, New York,
gift of Mourlot Frères.

2.14 Le Corbusier, *Le Corbusier poeme de l'angle Droit*, 1955.
Lithograph, 24¹/₂" x 15⁵/₈". Collection, Museum of Modern Art, New
York, gift of Berggruen & Cie.

Modern Handwritten Typography

Just as the style of the individual hand was brought to the
typography of the poster in the art nouveau period by the
influences of the fine arts, handcraft and handwriting as typography returned in the 1950s, largely also because of the
influence of fine artists. They recognized that typographic
elements could have a dual role as formal design elements and
symbols of communication. Pablo Picasso, Georges Braque,
Joan Miró, and the architect Le Corbusier all designed posters
for their own exhibitions, in which the style of typography
harmonized with the style of the image. Letterforms were drawn
with the same tool as the image was, and uninhibited handwriting as typography was appropriate to the images as well.

an appointment calendar with drawings from the collection of the museum of modern art

2.15 George Tscherny, 1958 appointment calendar cover for the Museum of Modern Art, New York, 1958.

Some of the artists appear to be flaunting the hand-written typography of their posters with a particularly irregular script or handcraft technique. This is true of Pablo Picasso's *Les Menines* poster and Le Corbusier's *Le Corbusier Poeme de l'Angle Droit* **(Figs. 2.13, 2.14)**. Both artists were excellent draftsmen, and lack of skill was definitely not a problem. The inconsistencies of Picasso's printed and script typography and Le Corbusier's hand-cut typography almost seem planned as an affront to the cold machine quality of set type and to the poster artists who use type rather than create it. The handcraft qualities of the typography served to set these posters and their creators apart from the other posters and poster designers of that time.

In *Le Corbusier Poeme de l'Angle Droit*, the hand-cut, irregular letterforms are in the same style as the image is and obviously were created by the same hand. In *Les Menines*, the same is true. The handwritten typography here is created with the same tool and line as the image is. In both cases the communication of the message is improved by the compositional unity and the novelty of the hand-generated typography. The use of letterforms created by an artist showing the same artistic skill in and sensitivity to typography seems a logical concept, but it was indeed new and innovative in the 1950s.

George Tscherny's 1958 appointment calendar for the Museum of Modern Art makes a visual connection between the typography on the cover and the function of the book **(Fig. 2.15)**. Appointment calendars are used to organize time, and the entries are handwritten and often doodled. The spontaneously drawn "'58" is a connection to both the function and the human hands that are to use it.

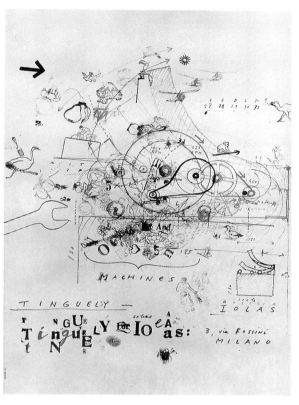

2.18 Jean Tinguely, *Machines Tinguely for Galerie Iolas*, 1966. Lithograph, 27½" x 19". Collection, Museum of Modern Art, New York, gift of Mr. and Mrs. Leo W. Farland.

Reudi Kulling's poster for Bic pens celebrates the handwritten word in the repeated strokes of the pen. The spontaneity and visual energy of the pen strokes communicate more clearly than any machine-produced typeface could **(Fig. 2.17)**. Free-flowing lines bleed off three edges of the poster, visually enlarging the poster format size and enhancing the movement of the pen strokes. The impulsive lines contrast dramatically with the photograph of the pen and the two other small typographic elements, "Bic" and " -.50."

Jean Tinguely used the same typographic style that he used in his drawings for a poster announcing an exhibition of his work **(Fig. 2.18)**. The letterforms are as fanciful as is the image, with some portions being carefully constructed and controlled and others free flowing. The poster imparts a feeling of collage in its combination of typographic sizes, weights, and colors. The repetition of the letterforms acknowledges the aural character of the typography when spoken. The name of the designer, Tinguely, is drawn again on top of the repetitive composition as if to reinforce the clarity of the repetitive written word.

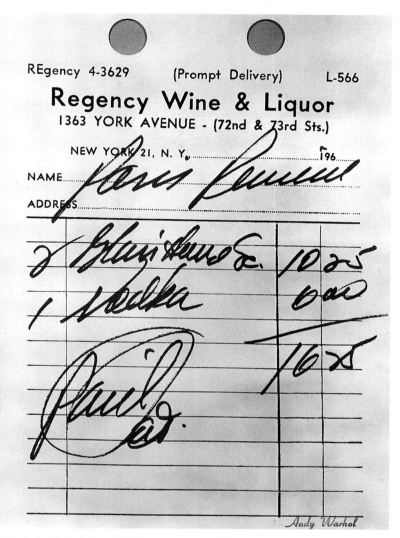

2.19 Andy Warhol, *Paris Review* poster, 1968. Silkscreen, 37" x 27". Collection, Museum of Modern Art, New York, gift of Page, Arbitrio and Resen.

The collagists of the early twentieth century defied convention when they made commonplace artifacts of everyday life such as ticket stubs, newspaper headlines, matchbook covers, and the like, part of the fine arts. Andy Warhol in the pop culture of the 1960s again defied convention and brought the commonplace to the level of art in his Campbell's Soup series. The same idea is at work in this poster, in which he uses a receipt as the background for his poster for *Paris Review* magazine and makes it an ironic part of his visual statement **(Fig. 2.19)**. The hard-edge lines of the receipt make an ideal contrast and appropriate background for the hastily scrawled handwritten typography. The final mocking touch is the artist's name rubber-stamped in the lower right corner.

2.20 Jim Dine, *City Center Gilbert & Sullivan* poster, 1968. Offset lithograph, 35" x 25". Collection, Museum of Modern Art, New York, gift of the designer.

2.21 Kazimierz Bascik, Solidarity identity, 1980.

In the *City Center Gilbert & Sullivan* poster, Jim Dine directly guides the viewer's eye by means of a strong vertical bar, to the face of the clown **(Fig. 2.20)**. The vertical stroke also guides the viewer's eye to the handwritten typography. Gilbert and Sullivan operas were written for the common people and were intended to be loved and enjoyed by everyone, and so too is the handwritten typography indicative of the masses. It acts as an invitation from one person to another to come and enjoy the opera. The sophisticated and esoteric notions of opera are dispelled by the handwriting and the clown imagery.

Major corporations spend millions of dollars on advertising campaigns to promote logo/product identification, yet this hastily scrawled visual symbol became well known worldwide and overnight because of the worthy cause and the power of the logotype **(Fig. 2.21)**. Solidarity is a Polish labor movement of ordinary working people, which is exemplified by the humble yet committed sincerity of the handwritten script and flag symbol. The bold, touching, and struggling letterforms represent the unity of people moving toward social justice with the flag raised.

Paul Davis is a well-known and talented illustrator who achieves compositional unity in his work by making the typography in his compositions as important and necessary as the image. There is a feeling of compositional cohesiveness in the work, and it is obvious that the typographic treatment is an integral part of the original concept and not an afterthought.

The graffitilike typography in the *For Colored Girls...* poster is appropriate to both the subject and a theatrical production **(Fig. 2.22)**. That is, the use of a graffiti style in communication acknowledges the urban environment where the play takes place. Furthermore, the graffiti is on a white tile subway wall, and the name and address of the theater is made part of a subway stop identification sign. The visual environment of the poster is convincing, and the viewer is mentally transported to a New York subway tunnel.

The *Threepenny Opera* poster typography appears to have been painted on hanging canvas behind the figure **(Fig. 2.23)**. The canvas forms a backdrop for the com-

2.22 Paul Davis, *For Colored Girls...* poster, 1975.

2.23 Paul Davis, *Threepenny Opera* poster, 1977.

position and the typography, which appears to have been recently painted. The soft brush strokes and drips impart a sense of careful yet just-finished work. The bowler hat on the foreground fugure overlaps a portion of the word *Opera*, yet the word is eminently legible. This overlapping of compositional elements serves to tie together the figure and typography as a compositional unit.

2.24. Roger Pfund, *Timbres et tampons d'artistes* poster, 1976.

2.25 Kimberly Elam, designer, Watson Riddle, letterer, Jazz Olympics identity, 1978.

The typography in *Timbres et tampons d'artistes*, Postmark and Rubberstamp Exhibition, by Roger Pfund is neither handwritten nor illustrated **(Fig. 2.24)**. Rather, it is stamped with an inked rubber stamp. The designer's hand is not seen in the way that the letterforms are created but in the designer's hand that applied ink and pressure to the stamp. The irregularity of the baseline and the repetitive impressions   producing the characters both allow the viewer to experience the process.

The problem of designing an identity for a jazz event is made all the more difficult because of the wide range of excellent design solutions for jazz events that preceded it. Irregular hand-drawn letterforms were chosen for this identity by Kimberly Elam and Watson Riddle to emphasize the spontaneous qualities of the music, which is often improvised and performed without a musical score **(Fig. 2.25)**. It seemed appropriate that the typography be "created without a score" as well, and existing typefaces were rejected for that reason.   Approximately twenty-five versions of the jazz letterforms were created by drawing with an india ink stopper. Then individual characters were selected from among them and cut and pasted together. A uniformity of style and proportion of thick to thin were the criteria used in the selection process. In the final version the letterforms were pasted in an artificial italic slant to emphasize the rhythm and movement of the music.

In Alan Fletcher's *Designer's Saturday* poster the playful shapes representing the basic elements of design—the circle, square, and triangle—become the playful images of kites and a balloon **(Fig. 2.26)**. These geometrically crafted elements are contrasted with both the hand-

2.26 Alan Fletcher, *Designers Saturday* poster, 1982.

2.27 Ivan Chermayeff, *Ivan Chermayeff: Works and Process*, one-man exhibition poster, Addison Gallery, 1984.

written typography and the linear shapes of the strings. The effect of these contrasts is further heightened by the format of a square within a rectangle and the overlapping of the square kite as it floats out of the format. The strings from the elements bleed off the page into the hands of the unseen designers. All the elements combine to form a visual sense of unity, playfulness, and enjoyment.

The hand-cut paper shapes and expressive handwriting are part of Ivan Chermayeff's personal style and visual approach to design **(Fig. 2.27)**. In this exhibition announcement poster there is a contrast between the handwritten typography and the cut edges of the paper shapes. The handwritten typography is "stuck" to the composition with a piece of brown mailing tape which becomes one of the visual elements. The carbon of a mailing receipt becomes another visual element. The semicircle has paperpunched areas, and the punch dots parade along the bottom of the composition. The idea of the collage of both found elements and handwritten message work together in a visual harmony of form and style.

2.28 James Cross and Steve Martin, *Connections* poster, 1984.

2.29 Poul Allan, *Visuel Kommunikation* self-promotional poster, 1985.

The *Connections* poster by James Cross and Steve Martin is an announcement for the Simpson Paper Company regarding the publication of a series of posters by distinguished designers **(Fig. 2.28)**. Rather than present a sequence of portraits, most of which would be unrecognized, or a series of typeset names, a series of signatures were collaged to announce the event and the participating designers. The designers' individual styles come through in the variety of signatures and styles which invite close inspection and conjecture as to the style each designer will use in the series. The problem of some of the signatures' illegibility is resolved by the further identification of small set typography beneath each signature. The color and quality of Simpson Paper is also displayed, as each signature is on a different color and variety of paper. Both the signatures and the torn paper scraps become the visual texture of the page which, although highly organized into a grid structure, is softened by the torn edges of the paper.

2.30 Michael Manwaring, *AIGA San Francisco* poster, 1984.

2.31 Roger Pfund, *Dessins genevois de Liotard à Hodler* poster, 1984.

Poul Allan uses a delightful play on words in his *Visuel Kommunikation* poster **(Fig. 2.29)**. A self-promotional poster for a visual communication designer, this work is designed to attract attention and to be displayed and enjoyed. The "kat" illustration uses hand-drawn repetitive and intense vertical lines to enhance the startled character of the image—so startled that its fur is flying. The handwritten typography is in perfect character and is composed with the same hand, media, and color as is the image. The introduction of the irregular letter spacing and handdrawn rule give the typography additional visual attention without overwhelming the image.

The collage effect of Michael Manwaring's *AIGA San Francisco* poster is heightened by the handprinted typography **(Fig. 2.30)**. The large capital *A* becomes an initial cap and a visual resting place, and the irregularity of the cut paper becomes a frame and a balancing surface edge for the struggling figure. The AIGA, the American Institute of Graphic Arts, is a professional organization of graphic artists and allied field professionals. The symbol of the AIGA is in the lower righthand corner. The poster makes a statement about the strug-

gles of the graphic designer during the design process, and the typography makes a strong visual reference to the feeling of creative immediacy and the handcraft qualities of the profession.

Graphic contrast is the most striking feature of Roger Pfund's *Dessins genevois de Liotard à Hodler* poster for an exhibition of drawings of the artist Liotard Hodler **(Fig. 2.31)**. The composition and colors are formal and symmetrical, with the typeset copy and images riding in a vertical column between two fine rules. The irregular handwritten typography is a beautiful contrast of the form and foreground compositional space with the symmetrical design. The blunt black crayon that was used to create the handwritten typography also contradicts the fine drawing instruments and delicate colors of the portraits on the poster. The balance and symmetry of the composition are emphasized by the use of the handwriting as a connotative reference to the artist's hand that created the images.

2.32 Alan E. Cober, *James Cagney* illustration, 1985.

2.33 Michael Schwab, *California* poster, 1985.

Alan Cober began to use handwriting in his illustrations for the *New York Times* in the 1970s and soon began to create whole campaigns with handwriting as typography. The handwritten typography in his *James Cagney* illustration forms a harmony of line and color with the visual image **(Fig. 2.32)**. Memorable lines from Cagney's films are inserted in the illustration and serve to jog the viewer's memory of the films. The viewer's eye moves around the composition by means of a more intense color treatment of the letters *a* and *g,* and of the jacket elbow and eye of the "victim" Cagney.

The vivid richness is established by the beautiful combination and control of color in Michael Schwab's *California* poster **(Fig. 2.33)**. The complementary contrast of the cool green and blue against the orange, pink, and purple against the yellow tones is compelling. The handcut typography on Schwab's poster is an extension of the same decisive handcut style that created the image. The typographic characters are simplified geometric forms. Vivid color is layered on vivid color to create a warm visual richness.

A major difficulty in designing posters for theatrical productions is creating a still image to convey at a glance the sense of story that takes several hours to perform on the stage. Bill Nelson and Ann Northington successfully collaborated to achieve that goal in their *Sweeney Todd* poster **(Fig. 2.34)**. The gruesome play *Sweeney Todd, the Demon Barber of Fleet Street* is reflected in the bold, undulating typography, which was created in about fifteen minutes by drawing on a paper towel with a magic marker. The upraised arms of the illustrated figures, holding a rolling pin and a straight razor, form a frame for the typography that emphasizes and anchors it as part of the composition. Alone, the typography would communicate a sense of the play's subject, but coupled with the illustration of two figures with demonic grins on their faces, the communication is intense and complete.

2.34 Bill Nelson, illustrator, Ann Northington, calligrapher, *Sweeney Todd* poster, 1985.

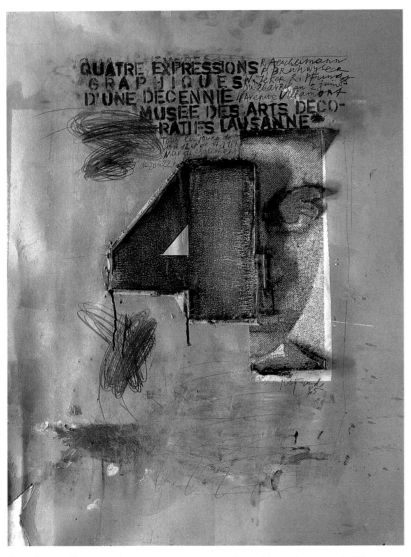

2.35 Roger Pfund, *4 Expressions graphiques d'une décennie* poster, 1985.

2.36 Everett Peck, *Mysterious Flaming Warrior* illustration, 1986.

The texture and placement of the typography in Roger Pfund's *4 Expressions graphiques d'une decennie* (Exhibition of the work of 4 graphic designers) is as important as are the texture and placement of the image **(Fig. 2.35)**. Pfund inscribed his typography into the painted surface of the poster, giving it depth and dimension. The typography provides the same feeling of texture and depth as does the image. The vigorous, repetitive stencil letterforms contrast with the handwritten script in carefully controlled and shaped areas of the composition. At first glance the typography may appear spontaneous, but further investigation reveals the tight compositional control. Spontaneous scribbles form additional textural areas that lend balance to the composition. There is no attempt to hide or cleanup the fingerprints that appear at the top of the composition: The designer wants the viewer to see and feel the hands that created the work. The construction of the dimensional foreground, the top typographic surface, the midground, the numeral four, and the background—with a mysteriously revealed portion of an illustration—demonstrate a work of intriguing dimension, shade, and shadow.

2.37 Tim Girvin, *American Music Week* poster for Maxell, 1986.

2.38 Frances Lovell, Michael Peters Group, *Coladiña Pineapple and Coconut Liqueur* package, 1986.

Everett Peck based his *Mysterious Flaming Warrior* illustration on a title from a Tom Mix cowboy film of the 1940s **(Fig. 2.36)**. Peck conjured up a fanciful image of a flaming Indian warrior on a flaming black stallion racing through the night. Both the title and illustration are mysterious and beautifully executed. Because the work was self-promotional, the illustrator had complete creative license with the type and image. The title typography is developed in a way that reflects the style and color of the imagery. A final touch is the curious handwritten typography at the very bottom: "He's Hard to Get Along With."

The names of different varieties of American music become the stripes on the flag in Tim Girvin's *American Music Week* poster **(Fig. 2.37)**. Nothing is more symbolic of America than its flag, and the handwritten textures of the words are reminiscent of the people from which they evolved. "Western, classical, gospel, country, choir" all are evocative of the region in which they originated and are a part of the American cultural fabric. The typography has a dual role as color texture and verbal informer. The rhythm of the handwritten typography accompanies the rhythms of the swaying flag. Just as the music has its origins in the grass roots of the country, so too does the handwriting.

The warm and easy life-style of tropical islands is reflected in the *Coladiña Pineapple and Coconut Liqueur* package by Frances Lovell **(Fig. 2.38)**. The handwritten typography is a personal invitation to enjoy the product. Unlike other liqueurs that have formal packages and associate themselves with mansions and evening dress, Coladiña implies beaches, sun, palm trees, and a casual life style. The images are as inviting and as colorful as the typography, and together they convey the essence of the product.

2.39 Roger Pfund, *Mars de Fritz Zorn* poster, 1986.

The *Mars de Fritz Zorn* poster by Roger Pfund is a seemingly spontaneous and uncontrolled composition, but when examined closely the hierarchical organization of the typography and image is tightly ordered and designed **(Fig. 2.39)**. Texture is a key element in the typography. Six typographic textures combine above and on the figure to form the composition and to organize the content of the message into six levels of communication, in order of importance. The shortened version of the title, Mars, is in the largest type, and it appears in the center of the poster overlapping the figure. The second level of typography is the full title, Mars de Fritz Zorn. The third level of typography is irregularly spaced stencil typography, Centre Culturel Suisse, composed with the negative spaces of the characters. The fourth level of typography is the identification of Festival d'automne á Paris 1986 and is done in a bolder style with more space around the characters. The fifth level of typography is the detailed information about the presentation directly above the figure. The sixth and final level of typography is a credit line for the designer and sponsor. The visual control over the seemingly spontaneous typographic elements and the image is a beautiful combination of design organizational principles, composition, and art.

Lilla Rogers was initially classically trained as a calligrapher and illustrator and for a time taught calligraphy. Finding the proscribed methods of calligraphy too limiting, she began to develop her own style of handwriting and to incorporate it into her illustration. In her *Dreamers in the Garden* the lyrical quality of the handwritten typography meshes appealingly with the set type **(Fig. 2.40)**. This piece is reminiscent of a Renaissance manuscript in which the first passages are highlighted and the text is begun with an initial cap.

The very structured format of the page, which includes a perimeter rule, magazine name and date, and two columns of copy divided by a vertical rule, contrasts with the unstructured handwritten typography. The composition of the handwritten typography acknowledges the structure of the page in the size and placement of the words. Readability is enhanced by means of with color changes, and the reader's eye is brought into the body of the text with the *I* initial cap as a cue. The combination of handwritten and set typography is stunning and is an excellent example of the potential of the handwritten word in publication design.

2.40 Lilla Rogers, *Dreamers in the Garden* illustration, 1986.

2.41 Everett Peck, *Art Direction* magazine cover illustration, 1987.

2.42 George Tscherny, San Francisco Clothing identity and shopping bag, 1987.

The tongue-in-cheek quality of Everett Peck's *Art Direction* cover brings an immediate visual response **(Fig. 2.41)**. The delightful combined abstract, surreal, and cubist quality of the figures is a statement about the art that is defined in the fuzzy speech bubble comment: "Pierre, Pierre, you are a hopeless realist!!" The same whimsical forms found in the imaginary imagery are reflected in the dimensional typography of the magazine's name, *Art Direction*. Artists and designers alike have a tendency to take themselves too seriously at times, and this work puts both in their place.

George Tscherny chose to use the quality of spontaneous street art by spray painting the *SF* identity for an avant-garde retail clothing store **(Fig. 2.42)**. The name of the store, San Francisco Clothing, is printed with a rubber stamp that has similar connotations of immediacy and handcraft. The fluorescent red identity on a pristine white bag makes it a difficult mark to miss or forget, and the shopping bags on the street and from a distance become portable advertisements for the San Francisco Clothing Company.

2.43 Tim Girvin, *Madness* illustration, 1987.

2.44 Tim Girvin, The Write Stuff *Status* cover, 1987.

The violent graphic emotion of Tim Girvin's *Madness* composition is testimony to the connotative visual power of the handwritten word **(Fig. 2.43)**. The finger-paint style is flowing with emotion. In striking contrast with this visual emotion is the "Write Stuff" calligraphy, which is harmoniously lyrical in form and style **(Fig. 2.44)**. The letterforms are controlled yet free flowing and generous. These two examples demonstrate the visual potential of handwritten typography as both a specific denotative communicator and a connotative communicator.

Graphologists (people who analyze handwriting) evaluate personality traits exhibited in letterform constructions and in the amount of pressure used in handwriting. Similarly, visual communicators can openly convey these traits through handwritten letterforms in a manner that allows any viewer to interpret the personality of the designer, the qualities of the subject, or the event described. Most type styles can only indirectly allude to connotative meaning. The designer's hand thus holds the answer to an infinite variety of communication problems, by the manner in which the handwritten word is constructed.

2.45 Lilla Rogers, *Truits Grenobles* illustration, 1988.

2.46 Lilla Rogers, *Sushi & Sashimi* illustration, 1987.

One of the reasons that Lilla Rogers began to use typography in her illustration is that her abstract style of drawing and painting was often interpretive and left much to the viewer's imagination. By reinforcing her visual images with handwritten titles and names, she was free to develop her abstract interpretive style, while still being able to communicate her message.

The deep-painted textures of *Truits Grenobles* extend to the letterforms that are an integral part of the composition (Fig. 2.45). The typography is as rich and textured as the images are, and both combine in a beautiful representation of the food's texture and its communication.

Rogers's *Sushi & Sashimi* illustration is done with watercolor, and the textures and tones of the medium are as harmonious and delicate as are the drawings themselves (Fig. 2.46). The style is reminiscent of Japanese brush painting but updated and expressionistic in style. It may be difficult to make raw fish and seaweed appealing to Westerners, but Rogers uses line and color to great advantage.

49

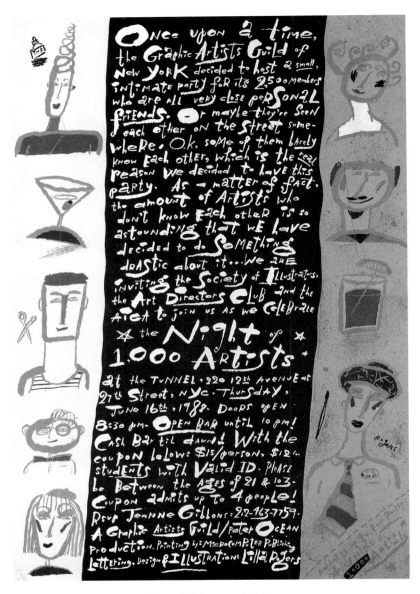

2.47 Lilla Rogers, Graphic Artists Guild poster, 1988.

Many of the most innovative and delightful works in this chapter—indeed, in this book—are the creations of artists, designers, or illustrators working free for an organization they believe in. Consequently, they can work with the stipulation that they have complete creative freedom. The resulting work can thus be even more inventive and interesting. Lilla Rogers's poster for the Graphic Artists Guild is an example of the free-flowing creativity that can result (Fig. 2.47). This poster is written in the style of a personal letter to the members of the guild to invite them and their contemporaries in the Society of Illustrators, the Art Directors Club, and the AIGA to a get-acquainted party entitled Night of 19,000 Artists. All of the organizations' members are involved in the visual arts and design, and thus the handwritten typography becomes a personal message and a tribute to their craft.

Experimental
Handwritten Typography

2.A Kimberly Elam, instructor, Karen Taylor, designer, Ned Heins, illustrator, *Underground Coffeehouse* composition, North Carolina State University, Department of Product and Visual Design, 1988.

2.B Kimberly Elam, instructor, Wade Dansby, designer, *Underground Coffeehouse* composition, North Carolina State University, Department of Product and Visual Design, 1988.

2.C Kimberly Elam, instructor, Kathleen O'Toole, designer, *Underground Coffeehouse* composition, North Carolina State University, Department of Product and Visual Design, 1988.

Students in design education often find it difficult to overcome the allure of set type, especially because setting type has become so easy with dry-transfer and desktop typesetting systems. Handwritten typography is regarded as something anyone can do, and thus too pedestrian for most students' tastes. This attitude is coupled with the fact that the emphasis on the hand skill of rendering type has largely disappeared from most design education, and many students believe that their handwriting skills are not fit for public visual consumption.

The experimental *Underground Coffeehouse* project is from a basic typography course **(Figs. 2.A** through **2.C)**. When the project was begun, the students were first asked to draw images of coffeepots and cups to be used in their design. Their first drawings looked like awkward efforts to approach photorealism. A discussion followed, which pointed out that if photography were desired, then the images should, indeed, be photographs. The image was to be visually interpretive, just as the handwritten typography would not attempt to mimic set type styles and would also be visually interpretive. A series of limited time contour and planar drawings yielded much better results.

In these projects the functional, verbal role of typography was reduced in favor of a much stronger and individual visual role. The style of the handwritten typography is in keeping with the illustration style, and the combination of the two assisted in unifying the compositions. Some works used typewritten typography as elements of contrast, and it was found that old fashioned strike-on typewriter type had visual connotations similar to those of handwriting, as the designer's hand is visible in the process. The resulting works were different in style and form from those of other typography projects but equally appropriate and much more expressive.

3.1 Pablo Picasso, *Guitar and Wine Glass*, 1912. Bequest of Marion Koogler McNay, McNay Art Museum, San Antonio, Texas. Copyright ARS N.Y./ SPADEM, 1988.

Chapter 3
Collage and Typography

Collage and Typography

Collage is both a method of composition and a means of creating typography. In collage composition, visual elements or objects that exist independently of one another are created or selected, cut or torn, and composed. Typographic collage for visual communication uses the same process of composition with letterforms and words, including the selection and combination of differing type styles, weights, colors, textures, and sizes in order to improve communication by means of contrast, juxtaposition, or tension.

The combination of collage composition and typographic messages reveals a symbolic and expressive quality beyond the communication content of a verbal message. Through collage, the impulsiveness of the designer's hand, the contrast of the selected elements, and the multiple layers of information and meaning are brought into a cohesive whole.

The Historical Context: Evolution from Cubism

The modern term *collage*, literally meaning pasted paper, evolved from the pasted-paper cubist compositions of the early twentieth century. Although the first known origins of collage compositions date from many centuries earlier, the modern collage movement is part of the cubist movement. Cubism, which began between 1906 and 1908 in Paris, revolutionized Western thought on the idea of abstract artistic representation. The compositional elements of color, space, form, and light were expressed by translating objects into abstract geometric planes viewed from many angles instead of a traditional single perspective view. A new visual language of form was created by this work, which defied classical representational composition, the principles of perspective, and the way in which art was interpreted by the viewer. Cubists attempted to reveal a different kind of reality, an expressive, interpretive reality of form, color, and texture.

Cubism reached its fullest expression by 1912. By then artists were searching for new forms of visual expression. Much of the subject matter in cubist painting, however, had become distorted and abstracted beyond recognition, and as a result there was a return to recognizable subjects. The cubists' earliest collages were preceded by paintings that attempted to simulate the texture of wood, marble, wallpaper, and other surfaces. Collage became a method by which new materials could be introduced into art.

The first collages were made in 1912 and are credited to the artists Pablo Picasso **(Fig. 3.1)** and Georges Braque. These collages consisted of commonly found objects such as wallpaper, newsprint, ticket stubs, packages, and cloth. For the first time, disposable elements of everyday life were incorporated into the fine arts: labels, fabrics, wrappers, newspapers, linoleum, and visiting cards. The use of common objects also represented a theoretical departure for the artists, in that their use of these materials challenged the social elitism of the fine arts, the traditional media of paint and ink, classical composition, and, of course, the fine arts' traditional representational subject matter.

When tracing a singular typographic movement, style, or method, as in this chapter's discussion of collage, it is difficult to focus on the subject without diverging to the influences that accompanied it. Sociologists, historians, psychologists, and art critics all have partial explana-

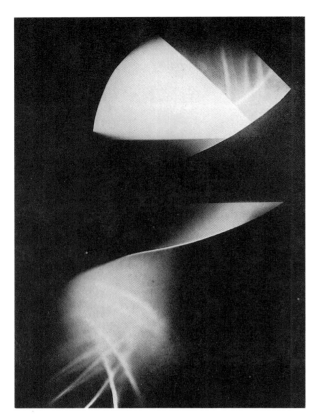

3.2 Lazlo Moholy-Nagy, *Fotogramm, vor/um*, appeared in *Foto-Qualität*, 1931. Courtesy of the Bauhaus-Archiv, West Berlin.

3.3 Lazlo Moholy-Nagy, *Foto-Qualität* cover, 1931. Courtesy of the Bauhaus-Archiv, West Berlin.

tions of collage. Our investigation of collage focuses primarily on the most compelling art movement that preceded it, cubism. However, at the same time it should be understood that futurism, suprematism, Dada, and de Stijl all were part of the influence on collage. Additionally, the Bauhaus was, as always, at the forefront of innovation, and the members of the Bauhaus were some of the first to experiment with collage and with the new technological means of photograms and photography in graphic design.

Typography in Collage

Most of these artists' found paper objects, especially wrappers, packages, and newsprint, contained typography, which accordingly gained significance in a fine arts medium. At first these objects were selected because of their color or texture, without concern for the words' verbal meanings. The visual energy of the typographic texture was regarded as an element of color and form and as a material of the machine age. Eventually, the typography was consciously manipulated to communicate the artists' social statements and, during the Russian Revolution, even propaganda. The presence of typography in collage meant that collage rapidly caught the attention of graphic designers and was readily translated into communication design.

Bauhaus Collage Translations

Some of the first evidence of collage influence in graphic design appeared in the early 1920s at the Bauhaus. It is here that the postcubist collage movement was translated from the fine arts into graphic design. The direct connection among experimental photograms, collage, and typography can be seen in the works of Moholy-Nagy **(Figs. 3.2, 3.3)**. The *Fotogramm* is one of many experimental works with photograms, beginning in the early 1920s. In the photogram compositions the elements of light and sensitized paper were the media. The reference to such experiments and the influence of collage were synthesized and directly applied to the title page for the journal *Foto-Qualität*. In this work a photograph, a photogram, and typography are collaged to form a single composition. Both the layering of compositional elements and the textured surfaces originated in collage. The display typeface, Futura Black, was designed at the Bauhaus as an interpretation of stencil typefaces, and its presence is reminiscent of collages with stenciled type. The difference between this work and conventional collage is the carefully organized and controlled imagery and typography which emphasizes the specific communication.

Assemblage

Kurt Schwitters, influenced by cubism, futurism, and Dadaism, developed his own approach to collage. Dubbing his work *Merz* from a scrap of typography revealed in one of his collages, his work focused on unifying compositions with found materials alone and rejecting earlier methods of drawing or painting in favor of collages so as to create cohesive compositions. This work expanded to include the technique of assemblage, a method of collaging both two- and three-dimensional objects. The influences in these early collage and assemblage compositions can be traced to the Bauhaus designers, who used a similar technique of composing with two- and three-dimensional elements for communication purposes.

An architect as well as a painter, photographer, and graphic designer, El Lissitzky was keenly aware of the compositional potential of both real and illusory three-dimensional space. Lissitzky adopted and employed constructivism and its philosophy of tectonics, the ideals of communism, texture, industrial materials, process, construction, and visual organization. Influenced by Kurt Schwitters's introduction of three-dimensional materials into collage, Lissitsky explored the introduction of illu-

3.4 El Lissitzky, Pelikan Ink window display for typewriter ribbons, 1924. Courtesy Verlag der Kunst, Dresden.

sory space into painting, an approach he called *Proun*. Prouns were, in Lissitzky's words, "the interchange station between painting and architecture."[1]

The Pelikan Ink window display model for typewriter ribbons combined constructivist ideals and Proun experimentation **(Fig. 3.4)**. The window display is organized much in the same way as is a poster with dimensional materials. The constructivist elements of the geometric circle, triangle, and rectangle are applied to enhance meaning. The circular saucer holds the typewriter ribbon product; the *p* is constructed from a rectangular bar and semicircle and holds the company logotype; and the triangle forms a guide and visual connection between the two shapes.

---

1. El Lissitzky, quoted by Philip B. Meggs, *A History of Graphic Design*, New York: Van Nostrand Reinhold, 1983, p. 312.

3.5 Ilia Zdanevitch, *ILIAzDE*, 1922. Lithograph 21 ³/₈" x 19 ¹/₈". Collection, The Museum of Modern Art, New York. Arthur A. Cohen Purchase Fund.

The influences of both collage and Dada can be seen in Ilia Zdanevitch's *ILIAzDE* poster **(Fig. 3.5)**. The vertical rules that divide the sections of the poster almost appear to be the irregular edges of cut pieces of paper pasted onto the composition. The sections of the poster change in texture as the type size varies and the copy changes from upper and lowercase to caps. Concessions are made to legibility, as the sectioning of the poster divides the French-language copy from the Russian-language copy, and a map is included to direct the viewer.

El Lissitzky's typographically collaged *Merz-Matinéen* composition **(Fig. 3.6)** was done in collaboration with Kurt Schwitters. The design is a beautiful combination of the Merz and constructivist ideals. Merz sought to unify composition through the use of color, form, and texture. Constructivist ideals advocated the unification of communist philosophy, materials and technology, and visual organizational principles. The composition's visual activity intensifies according to whether the typography reads from left to right, top to bottom, or bottom to top, and it also changes the direction of the letterforms, as in the word *progra2m*. Because of the organized and structured visual environment, the playful combinations of textures, images, and typography form a visual unity that clearly communicates. Rather than fight the vertical/ horizontal lockup system of the letterpress, Lissitzky works with it as well as with the printers' ornaments of rules, hand, and egg shape.

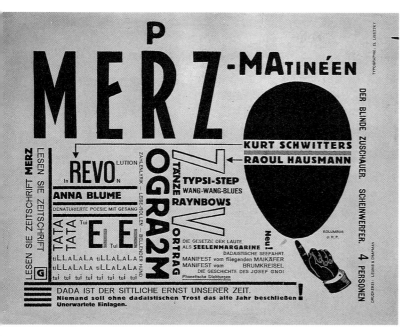

3.6 El Lissitzky, *Merz-Matinéen* program cover, 1923. Letterpress, 9" x 11".
Collection, The Museum of Modern Art, New York. Gift of Philip Johnson.

3.7 Henryk Berlewi, *Mechano=Fakturowych*, 1924. From the collection of Merrill C. Berman, New York City.

Collage and Stencil Typography

In the early 1920s Henryk Berlewi investigated the elimination of illusory three-dimensional elements and the mechanization or fusion of visual communication design with the industrial age. Working with only a restrained palette of three colors (red, black, and white), geometric forms, and typography, he organized elements based on mathematics. The *Mechano = Fakturo-wych* (Mechanical = Reproduction), a result of these experiments, is composed entirely of stencil typography and nonobjective imagery **(Fig. 3.7)**. Rather than selecting, cutting, and collaging or pasting paper, Berlewi selected a variety of sizes and styles of stencil masks and painted red and black gouache through them. The seemingly intuitive placement of the collage elements and the stencil typography is in reality a complex mathematical composition.

The techniques of typographic generation by means of stencil typography and composition with collage are closely linked by the ways in which they are commonly used, and they are frequently found to be used in tandem. Stencil typography is created by dabbing paint through a paper or metal mask, and it was originally used in commerce to label crates for shipment and later by the military as a means of rapid identification. Just as the materials of collage were the materials of everyday life, so too were the stencil letterforms. Each method, collage and stencil typography, has strong connotations of a spontaneous communication medium and dynamic contact with the surface. This compelling feeling of visual impulse of both form and placement reveals the existence of the designer's hand in the development of the composition. Commonality is also evident in the way in which the work is frequently constructed: the spontaneous placement of typographic and image elements and the combinations of color, texture, and contrast of elements and ideas.

3.8 A. M. Cassandre, *L'Intransigeant*, 1925. Photo courtesy of the Reinhold–Brown Gallery, New York City.

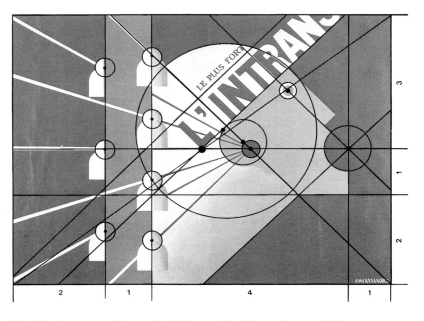

3.9 Visual structure diagram, A. M. Cassandre, *L'Intransigeant*, 1925.

Influence of Cassandre

A. M. Cassandre was an unusually successful translator of the fine arts into design. Cassandre, a pseudonym for Adolphe Jean-Marie Mouron, was able to synthesize in his work avant-garde art and popular commercial appeal. Using the simplified, stylized imagery of the cubists and the compositional qualities of collage, he was able to translate representational form into powerful visual symbols. The simplicity of his work, coupled with a keen sense of compositional unity, contributes to the visual power of many of his posters. This approach directly contrasted with the very decorative work of most of the poster designers of that time and thus served to set Cassandre apart as an extraordinary innovator.

In Cassandre's poster, *L'Intransigeant*, designed in 1925, the influences of Braque and Picasso can be seen in the stylized manner in which the head of the figure is constructed and in the flat space occupied by the figure and telegraph pole **(Fig. 3.8)**. Similar to that of the cubists as well is Cassandre's restrained color palette. The references to collage are found in the way that the typography is handled as portions of separate visual elements that are selected, cut, and composed with the imagery. The abbreviation of the newspaper's masthead inscription, "Le Plus Fort Tirage des Journaux de Soir," into LE PLUS FORTE, is similar to collage typography in which only portions of words are revealed. *L'Intrans*, as well, is an abbreviation for *L'Intransigeant*, the name of the newspaper. Positive and negative space provide the same elements here as overlapping elements do in collage.

A master of the pragmatic use of visual theory, Cassandre organized his composition around the three circles in the composition: the eye, ear, and mouth **(Fig. 3.9)**. The same concentric circles for eyes can be seen in some of Léger's cubist paintings, which were created in the previous decade. The repetitive proportions of the composition, approximated in the visual structure diagram, achieve maximum asymmetry and compositional unity. Each element has a purposeful size, position, and interrelationship to all of the other elements on the page.

In Cassandre's poster, *Wagon Bar*, the cubist and collage influences are keenly felt, and the experiments of collage and photography are realized **(Fig. 3.10)**. The images of the seltzer bottle, glass and straws, wine bottle, glass, train wheel, and bread loaf are composed on layer after layer of compositional space. The image size, placement, and color draw the viewer's eye back through the composition. The hand-drawn elements

3.10 A. M. Cassandre, *Wagon Bar* poster, 1932. From the collection of Merrill C. Berman, New York City.

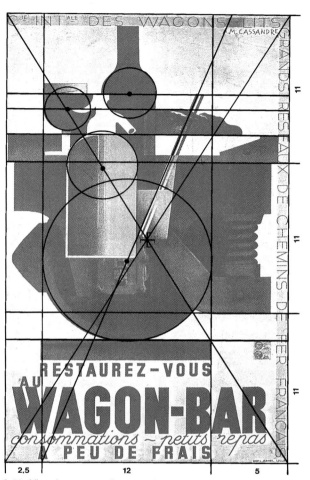

3.11 Visual structure diagram, A. M. Cassandre, Wagon Bar poster, 1932.

appear to be on flat planes, flatter still because of the contrast with the obvious dimensional reality of the photograph of the train wheel.

The visual analysis of this poster reveals the complex visual interrelationships of the elements and the tight, compositional control of their placement **(Fig. 3.11)**. The circle, a favorite compositional element of Cassandre, appears four times: most obviously in the wagon wheel and then more discreetly in the radiused shoulders of the seltzer bottle, the shoulders of the wine bottle, and the bottom bowl of the wineglass. A line from the center of the wineglass circle to the center of the seltzer bottle circle forms a diagonal from the left top corner to the bottom right corner. The center of the wine bottle circle to the center of the train wheel circle form a vertical line through the center of the track and the justified typography under the track. The diagonal from the straws in the glass touches the upper right corner and the lower left corner of the block of justified typography. The propor-

tions of the visual areas are repeated horizontally and vertically. Clearly, the construction of the elements, their placement on the page, and the interrelationships of form are the result of an exceptional and deep understanding of compositional theory and its practice.

The manner in which Cassandre successfully translated avant-garde ideas into popular poster communications had a profound effect on the development of graphic design. The translation of complex visual subjects into symbolic form became a part of the program at the Bauhaus. The integration of the typography and architectonic visual organizational systems into the composition also became a goal. Control of the composition, elements, and placement were hallmarks of Cassandre's work. Now the dynamic irregularity of fine arts collage was replaced in design with the precision and restraint of the machine age. This ultimately served to separate further the fine arts from design.

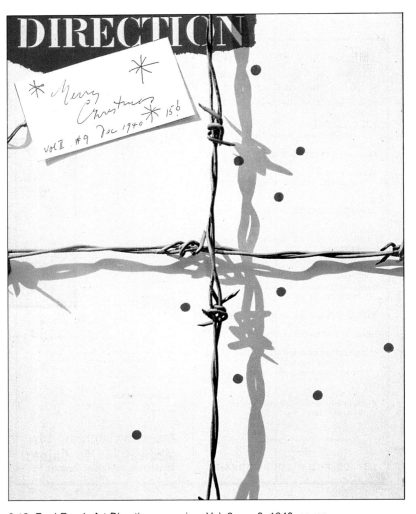

3.12 Paul Rand, *Art Direction* magazine, Vol. 3, no. 9, 1940, cover.

Throughout his career, Paul Rand has been strongly influenced by fine arts movements and artists. His ability to understand art and design and their congruent aspects as well as their differences has enabled him to bring a sense of vision to the profession and practice of visual communication design. His Christmas 1940 cover for *Art Direction* magazine shows evidence of collage **(Fig. 3.12)**. The compositional elements are simple yet direct and effective in symbolic meaning and composition. That is, during December 1940 all of Europe was at war, and the tension and fear are symbolized by the elements collaged on the cover. The circles can be readily interpreted as a smattering of bullet holes and the barbed wire as package "ribbon" or perhaps a Roman cross. The magazine title is exposed by tearing away a portion of the white cover to reveal a symbolic blood red ground and stencil typography, which in this context has strong military connotations. The final ironic touch and gripping contrast is the Christmas package tag with the cheerful sentiment, "Merry Christmas." This cover was prophetic, as a year later the United States entered the war.

The combination of geometric elements, photographed elements, torn paper, handwriting, and stencil typography are precisely the kind of mix that the collagists used in fine arts composition. Rand was able to compose these elements with the soul of a artist and the mind of a communicator.

Modern Collage and Typography

The accessibility and common use of rational, hard edged letterforms in graphic design has removed the hand of the designer from the viewer's perception. Many visual communications appear as if they were created impassionately by a computer, and the visual connotations are cold, informational, and rational. Collage, on the other hand, is closely tied in the viewer's mind with an art form and is directly related to the human qualities of art. As a communication medium, collage reveals personal expression, impulsiveness, and human irregularity, all desirable traits in the rational computer age.

Collage is a method by which multiple layers of communication are combined to become a unified message. The process can occur in a single word to bring together a number of visual symbols or interpretations within a single verbal message or, in a broader context, in a complex arrangement of symbolic visual and verbal elements. Because of these compositional attributes, collage is an excellent visual and verbal medium for graphic design.

Modern collage composed by graphic designers contains compositional qualities similar to those of the early collage artists, with the added task of specific communication. Contrast of form or juxtaposition of ideas is a trait that designers still use to clarify meaning. Just as the first collagists returned to representational imagery from abstraction, the modern collage of graphic design has returned to its early compositional roots from modern, rational organization. The importance that the early collagists placed on multiple-plane compositions and the play of light, color, surface, form, and texture all are a part of modern collage and can be controlled and emphasized even more through computer technical reproduction processes.

Some of the most dynamic qualities of collage are reflected in painter Larry Rivers's poster for the *First New York Film Festival* **(Fig. 3.13)**. It is interesting that a return to collage-style composition in visual communication design was initiated by a fine artist, as the first graphic design collages were made by individuals originally trained as fine artists. It is also interesting that the typography is as impulsive in form, color, and placement as is the hand-drawn imagery. In this poster the type and image have a direct relationship to each other in the style in which they are drawn and then worked into a unified composition. Frequently, visually active works with many shapes and textures have difficulty communicating a message. Rivers solved this problem by controlling the viewer's eye through the isolation of the typography in three areas. He then used a hierarchical system of size, in which the title is the largest and most important element. Next, the second level of typography is a circle for visual emphasis. Finally, touches of color highlight the three typographic groups. These three groups of typography form a unifying triangular shape, and the typography at the bottom is placed horizontally as a stabilizing influence.

The visual excitement initiated by the rough-textured letterforms contrasts with the machine-generated typography of most other design communications of the time. This poster also differs from others of that era in that the pictorial image usually would be separated from the typography. This separation would occur both in the placement on the page and in the difference in the style of the typography, as opposed to the image. *The First*

3.13 Larry Rivers, *First New York Film Festival 1963* poster, 1963.

3.14 Larry Rivers, *Selected Poems of Frank O'Hara*, book cover, 1975.

3.15 Milton Glaser, *Polish Poster* poster, 1968.

New York Film Festival poster, with its contradiction of the graphic design norms of the time, is almost a defiant work by a fine artist. The technical, rational qualities of visual communication pale in the visual excitement of the dynamic, artistic qualities of the human hand, eye, and mind.

Rivers again used collage in the design of a book jacket cover for *Selected Poems of Frank O'Hara* **(Fig. 3.14)**. The drawing of the artist is composed on brown paper and then trimmed and pasted in place. The stencil typography is created with the same line quality as are the drawing, the words, and the image, thereby creating a harmonious relationship. Through these elements, a powerful statement is made about the honesty and sincerity of the poet and poetry. Rivers was able to see beyond the expected and the ordinary into the heart and soul of the poet and to communicate this through his work.

Originally trained as an illustrator, Milton Glaser was not content to work solely in a single discipline. Rather, his work embraces all forms of communication design, and his compositions have a strong visual concept and a

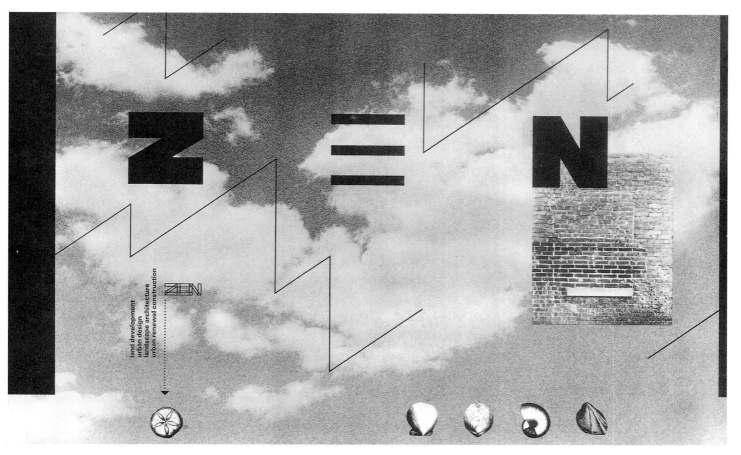

3.16 Greg Thomas, *Zen* poster for a Japanese architectural firm, 1978.

unity of all elements. Because of Glaser's multidisciplinary vision, his solutions to problems reflect unique and unconventional approaches. In his poster for an exhibition of Polish posters, Glaser's concept reflects the poster's city-street orientation, which is still prevalent in Poland **(Fig. 3.15)**. Using the collage forms of ripping and tearing paper, earlier messages below the surface are revealed. This technique is reminiscent of the street-poster surface which holds layer after layer of posters, with an occasional glimpse of history.

Zen, according to *The American College Dictionary*, "advocates self-contemplation as the key to understanding the universe." This sense of mystical contemplation is visually realized in Greg Thomas's *Zen* poster **(Fig. 3.16)**. The collage of the natural environment and man-made materials is filled with symbolism. A cloud-filled sky is the backdrop and unifying force for a variety of elements: a brick wall, seashells, and the typography and zig zag rules. The sky can be seen as symbolizing the universe. The brick wall represents man-made building materials. Seashells have mathematically proportioned structures, a motif often repeated in architecture. This poster invites contemplation. For example, the *z* and *n* are exactly the same typographic character turned on edge. The *e* is reduced to three parallel bars with the negative spaces forming an equal sign.

Anton Schöb
Buchdruck--Offsetdruck
Foliendruck
Birchstrasse 102
8050 Zürich
Telefon 01-311 22 60

Seit April 1981 steht
in unserem Betrieb die neue Fotosatz-
anlage: Ein Texterfassungssystem
«Grafitex CDS-400» mit on-line
verbundenem Kathodenstrahlbelichter
«Compugraphic cg 8600».
Zurzeit haben wir rund 30 Schriften in
direktem Zugriff. Diese belichten wir in
½-Punkt-Abstufungen von 4 bis 72 Punkt.
Dank neuem Digitalisierungsverfahren
geschieht dies ohne «Sägezahn-Effekt».
Verlangen Sie Schriftmuster.

3.17 Rosmarie Tissi, *Fotosatz* poster, 1981.

The texture of the sky serves to hold and bind these many elements into a cohesive composition. The vertical strokes of the zig zag rules align with the edges of the typographic elements and with the other objects in the composition. This poster is compositionally ordered, symbolically conceived, and visually realized.

Rosmarie Tissi regards letterforms and blocks of copy as individual elements existing on their own planes and free to move in space in front of or behind other elements. Letterform textures and the visual power of negative space are at work in her *Fotosatz* (Photo type-setting) composition **(Fig. 3.17)**. The letterforms shift from plane to plane in the compositional space, from positive to negative representation, and from solid to textured form. The movement and differences in space, plane, and texture are arranged through a controlled collage process. The designer's skill is evidenced by her use of several letterform changes while maintaining the integrity and readability of Fotosatz. The diagonal red bar, "Für die Zukunft" (For the future) anchors the composition and gives the viewer's eye a resting place within all of the visual activity. The work is further unified in that the diagonal of the stripes in the *F*, the diagonal of the dots in the *z*, and the "Für Die Zukunft" diagonal all are at a common angle.

Tissi's *Sommer Theater* poster offers strong contrasts of form **(Fig. 3.18)**. Rather than forcing the descriptive copy into a rectangular shape or hiding the shape on a white background, the copy block shape is determined by the rag, irregular right or left edges, of the typeset copy, in much in the same way that the eye perceives textures of type. These shapes become an irregular texture that marches down the page around the sun. The smooth geometric construction of the circular sun shape and the bars holding the words *Sommer Theater* are at variance with the irregular copy blocks. Movement in space occurs when the copy blocks overlap the horizontal "Theater" bar.

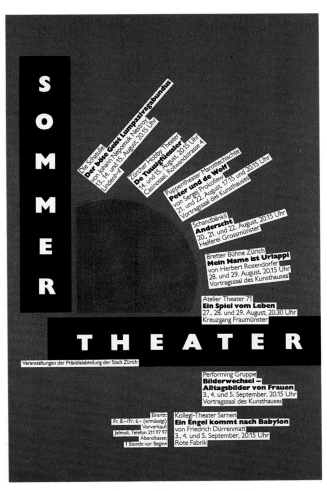

3.18 Rosmarie Tissi, *Sommer Theater* poster, 1981.

3.19 Rosmarie Tissi, *Offset* poster, 1981.

A tribute to the Tissi's control of compositional space is the clear way in which the *Offset* poster reads **(Fig. 3.19)**. The title's letters are turned 90 degrees and are cropped by overlapping. The compositional space is the controlling force, with the *o* composed of geometric circles without the need for baseline orientation. The *o* as a circular form is the most compelling element and the natural starting point. The *f* letterforms move the eye back in space and bring it back to the foreground with the front *s*. Once again the eye is guided back in space with the overlapping *e* and *t*. The small blocks of type and their cutout shapes mirror the forms of the *f*, *e*, and *t*, as well as contrast with the curvilinear forms. This control of compositional space adjusts, guides, and orients the manner in which the poster is read, to make it both logical and visually stimulating.

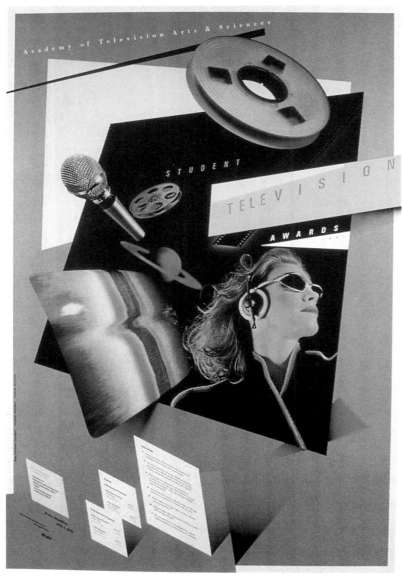

3.20 April Greiman and Jayme Odgers, *Academy of Television Arts & Sciences Student Television Awards* poster, 1981.

An achievement of compositional skill and current technology, April Greiman's and Jayme Odgers's poster for the Academy of Television Arts & Sciences, demonstrates the current potential of collage **(Fig. 3.20)**. The foreground compositional window of gray space inside the white perimeter stripe is pierced still further by another angled window into deep space. The format is energized as the planes bleed off the edge of the poster on the sides and bottom left corner. There is a sense of the elements' dynamic movement as a film reel moves across the composition, and the microphone moves out of the pierced window as the multicolored plane of a television screen moves in. The subordinate copy is portrayed as free-standing, dimensional pieces of paper.

The play with space, shape, and typography makes this poster an exciting and stimulating visual statement. The designers' knowledge and sensitivity to compositional space, as well as their familiarity with the visual theory and technology to manipulate illusory space, is evident.

Dementos is a musical about a group of social outcasts who live on the streets, in welfare hotels, or in low-rent housing. These people are regarded by others in society as demented, or *dementos*. The logo was designed by illustrator Ron Lieberman, to "communicate a feeling of street art and graffiti." Some letterform shapes were inspired by neon signs and the other characters are represented by hand-drawn scrawls **(Fig. 3.21)**. A final touch to the logo is a spray-painted negation line that crosses out the entire word, symbolizing the unwillingness of society to acknowledge the *dementos* segment of society. The poster was designed to communicate isolation, despair, and feelings of being trapped. The multiple levels of the human personality are revealed in the lower right-hand corner where three images are combined: Chains, chain-link fencing, and a guard dog represent the feeling of being imprisoned by circumstance.

Collage is an ideal medium for communicating such potent and complex subject matter. The texture of the spray-painted elements and the carelessly ripped edges becomes an ideal way to reveal the depth of despair. The primary level of communication is achieved with the visually descriptive identity. In the secondary level of information, only small portions of the images are revealed, causing the viewer to

3.21 Ron Lieberman, *Dementos* poster for Duval/Leigh and Because Productions, 1981.

examine closely all of the bits and pieces and mentally make the connections. The third level of communication is the small typeset specific information. The symbolism of the logo and the selected elements is individually strong and combined becomes a forceful composition.

Roger Pfund's *Abonnement 83–84* (Subscription 83–84) poster brings the viewer into the environment of a playhouse through the illusion of illumination by a theater spotlight **(Fig. 3.22)**. This spotlight shows information about a series of five avant-garde plays that will be presented during the theatrical season. The typography consists of individually cut letterforms that are pasted together on obviously drawn baselines. The letterforms are closely cropped and crowded together to convey a feeling of tension and urgency. Essentially a composition in black and white, the name of the theater is emphasized through the use of red typography on a black ground. Subordinate information regarding the dates appears to be rubber-stamped in red at a contrasting diagonal to the black typography. As with many of Pfund's other posters, texture is an important aspect of the composition, and in *Abonnement* the dense texture of the crowded black letterforms and the dimensional texture of the surface of the cut letterforms are important to the connotative feelings of the poster.

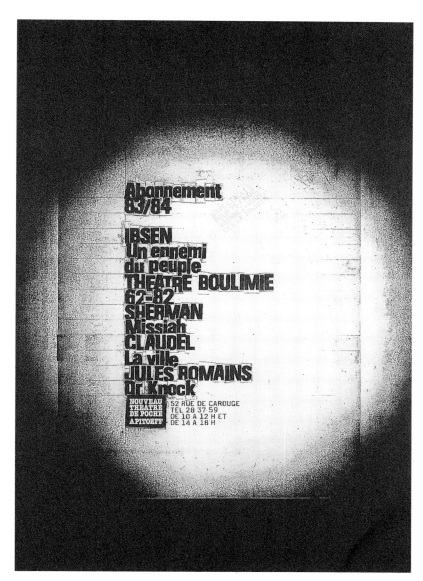

3.22 Roger Pfund, *Abonnement 83–84* poster, 1983.

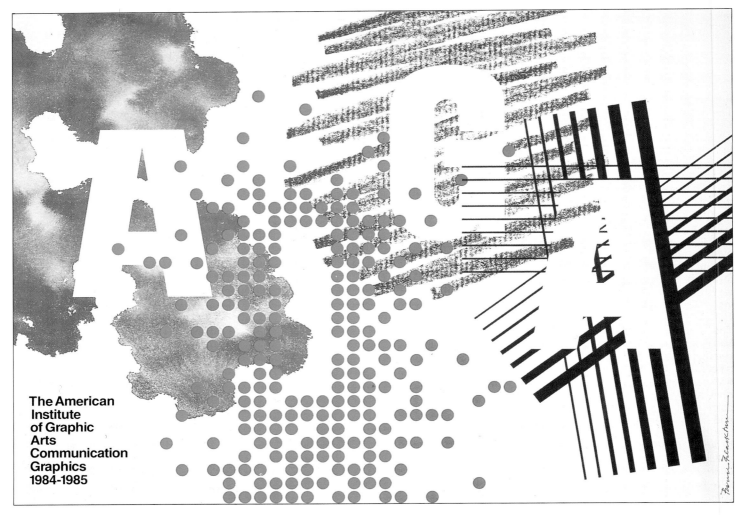

The American
Institute
of Graphic
Arts
Communication
Graphics
1984-1985

3.23 Bruce Blackburn, *AIGA* poster, 1984.

The poster for the AIGA by Bruce Blackburn uses the negative space of the four textures to reveal the letters AIGA **(Fig. 3.23)**. They are formed from a combination of creative processes: hard-edged, ruled lines; hand-drawn, scribbled lines; machine-made, circular bullets; and a handmade, watercolor texture. The AIGA, American Institute of Graphic Arts, is an organization of graphic artists and allied professionals. The concept of describing the organization with a series of textures and colors refers to the many different people, media, and styles that comprise the group. The fact that the textures overlap enforces the idea of unifying different elements. The technique of layering unrelated elements is similar to that of collage, and the irregular placement of the textures, although highly controlled, is visually stimulating.

The explosion of color initially greets the viewer in Michael Bierut's *AIGA NY* poster **(Fig. 3.24)**. The positive and negative portions of the bright yellow and green typography and backgrounds on the poster are mixed with selective tearing that reveals portions of the color-reversed typography underneath. The intensity of the color is heightened with a diagonal, hand-drawn yellow and blue texture at the top and irregular scribbles in black. One of the scribbles places a hand-drawn heart between AIGA and NY to create another message, "AIGA Loves NY." The designer retains visual control by taping a bright blue typeset piece of paper with specific information near the bottom of the poster which becomes a visual resting place. The vibrant blue, green, and yellow form a striking yet harmonious, analogous color scheme that is intensified by the black ground at the bottom of the poster. Though appearing impulsive, this poster is very carefully controlled in order to communicate information from the broad to the specific to the suggested.

3.24 Michael Bierut, *AIGA NY Events Autumn 1984*, 1984.

3.25 Michael Manwaring, *SantaCruz American-in-Paris series*, Fall 1984.

3.26 Michael Manwaring, *SantaCruz American-in-Paris series*, Fall 1984.

3.27 Michael Manwaring, *SantaCruz American-in-Paris series*, Fall 1984.

Michael Manwaring used collage as a main theme for his campaigns for SantaCruz fashions **(Figs. 3.25** through **3.30)**. The campaigns are centered on the SantaCruz identity, designed by Manwaring, which, unlike most static and inflexible identity designs, readily changes in color, texture, and position. Consisting of italic type in a contrasting color, the background changes in texture and color to suit the color on the page or to identify a particular group

3.28 Michael Manwaring, *SantaCruz MTV* poster, 1984.

3.29 Michael Manwaring, *SantaCruz Summer* series, 1984.

3.30 Michael Manwaring, *SantaCruz Summer* series, 1984.

of materials. From diagonal stripes to dots to plus signs, the texture changes, as does the color, in order to form a flexible identity system. The identity is immediately recognized because of the consistent type style and triangular shape designed to fit comfortably into a corner of any application. The torn white edge of the identity serves to separate it from the other colors and textures used on the many promotional pieces. The established visual theme of the identity as an element of collage is followed through consistently on all promotional materials.

The identity system and the collaged compositions communicate the company's goal of current fashions, youthful playfulness, and cutting-edge design. Just as this identity invites a variety of interpretations, so too does the collage format, from the image-rich summer series to the sophisticated and restrained American-in-Paris series.

3.31 Roger Pfund, *Knock de Jules Romains* poster for Nouveau Théâtre de Poche, Geneva, 1984.

3.32 Ronald Ridgeway, *Ridgeway Ave. Ridgeway Ct* illustration, 1986.

Less painterly and more constructed than other posters by Roger Pfund, *Knock de Jules Romains* uses the harsh-cut edges of the paper to define the visual elements on the page **(Fig. 3.31)**. The severity of the hacked-out letterforms and the obvious manner in which they are glued to the page have a visual harshness that is related to the subject matter of surgical malpractice. The color shapes are cut out with equal severity, forming a composition of abrupt, irregular edges. Other collage elements include an engraving of the human musculature and a table of crude, medieval surgical instruments.

One of the rules of thumb in collage composition is that the more numerous and varied the elements are, the more difficult it will be to achieve communication and compositional unity. Too many elements all demanding attention at once can cause the viewer's eye to move continuously around the page and become distracted by the visual activity, thus hampering the communication of a specific message. Ronald Ridgeway is an illustrator who has mastered the balancing of many collage elements into cohesive compositions **(Figs. 3.32** through **3.34)**.

3.33 Ronald Ridgeway, *FE* cover illustration, *Is Your Thinking Analog or Digital?* 1985.

3.34 Ronald Ridgeway, DuPont Sports Products illustration, *Ahead of the Game,* 1986.

In the self-promotional *Ridgeway Ct.* collage, the scraps and pieces of a busy illustrator's life are portrayed with torn and cut bits of photos, photocopies, maps, and drawn and painted elements. The path of his workday, from home in Montclair, New Jersey, to work in Manhattan, New York, and back home again is traced by a visually directive line that changes color and texture but whose triangular shape binds together all of the fragmented elements into a unified visual message. With simple, recognizable, and personal elements, Ridgeway succeeds in elevating his daily life to a higher level, one of importance, dignity, and excitement.

Symbolic color and images are used to express the two forms of thinking in the *Is Your Thinking Analog or Digital?* illustration. The generic person is in silhouette expressing the commonality to all people of the two modes of thinking. The digital side images are in black and white with straight-cut edges and represent the quantitative thought made up of money, numbers, graphs, and keyboards. The analog images are in color, with the edges softened by tears, and they form the creative aspects of thinking, including art, music, dance, and philosophy. The relatively equal size of the images assists in balancing the composition. Because the illustration is symmetrically organized, the viewer's eye moves through it and back to the center and finally rests on the image of the seashell.

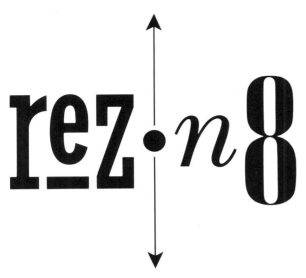

3.35 John Weber, *Rez,n8* identity, 1987.

Typographic messages offer three levels of communication: verbal, visual, and vocal. In John Weber's *Rez,n8* identity (pronounced resonate) the level of the word's verbal communication and its deciphering is reduced in favor of increasing communication on the visual and vocal levels **(Fig. 3.35)**. The rebus quality of this identity invites interpretation and participation. The numeral is a visual substitution changing the way that the identity is interpreted, with its meaning discovered from vocal sound. This exercise links the identity with the actual meaning of the word *resonate* from *The American Collegiate Dictionary*: "To amplify vocal sound by the sympathetic vibration of air in certain cavities and bony structures." This identity system was designed for a computer animation house. The collage of the playful typographic and nonobjective identity elements underscores the meaning and alludes to the quality of symbolic interpretation and movement in computer animation.

3.36 John Weber, *Printbox* identity, 1988.

The Printbox identity was designed for a firm that produces video manipulation for print-media publications **(Fig. 3.36)**. Here the verbal and visual levels of communication are increased to clarify meaning. The collaged typographic elements of serif and sans serif types, outline and pixelated types, and symbolic and hand-drawn characters have strong visual connotations that relate to the many different forms of visual expression or combinations of expressions also offered by the firm. The verbal qualities of the letterforms are retained, resulting in clear, concise communication.

SHAKESPEARIENCE

3.37 Mark Burn, *Shakespearience* typography, 1987.

The *Shakespearience* identity by Mark Burn also uses collage to enhance the visual meaning of the typography **(Fig. 3.37)**. The variety of letterforms offers individual symbols in connection with the many interpretations and values of the plays of William Shakespeare. Collage in identity design conveys an understanding of the use of letterforms as specific symbols of communication, combined with the symbolic interpretation of form.

3.38 Eight Five Zero, *The Guitar and Other Machines* album sleeve for the Durutti Column, 1987.

3.39 Gordon Salchow, ATP Tennis poster, 1988.

On the album sleeve for the Durutti Column, layers of semitransparent images and type form the message **(Fig. 3.38)**. The perspective technique of the texture gradient is used to give images the illusion of existing in deep space. Blurring or out-of-focus techniques are gradually sharpened to bring the elements closer to the viewer. The viewer's eye is led from deep background space and the shadow image of the electric guitar to midground space and the detailed photographic image to the closest element, the guitar. A transparent ground bar is used to highlight the word *guitar*, and to increase its legibility and importance. The rule device is used yet again to enforce the supporting typography leading the viewer's eye throughout the typography.

Gordon Salchow's *ATP Tennis* poster is a complex collage of photographs, textures, and colors **(Fig. 3.39)**. The large scale ATP letterforms establish the central structural theme for the poster, with all of the other elements related to these three letters. The letterforms and textures are in flat foreground space that contrasts with that of the photographed images. The photographed images are tightly cropped details of the game and move the viewer's eye from the foreground of typography and texture to small windows of deep space. The negative space occupied by the tennis racket is a delightful visual surprise, with the implied strings changing the texture of the *t*.

3.A Stan Brod, instructor, Mona Leonard, student designer, Visual interpretation of the subject *humanity*, University of Cincinnati, Graphic Design Department.

3.B Katherine McCoy, instructor, Robert Nakata, designer, *Jaugeon* typographic history poster, Cranbrook Academy of Art, 1985.

Collage has many compositional attributes that make it an excellent visual and verbal medium for experimentation by design students. Particularly in the design of complex messages, collage is a method by which multiple layers of communication can be combined to become a unified message. The process can occur in a single word to bring together a number of visual symbols or interpretations, or in a broader context in a complex arrangement of symbolic visual and verbal elements. As the complexity of collage composition increases, visual control is achieved only through careful planning and structuring. If not, the resulting work will be a garbled message of visual noise.

The humanity composition by student designer Mona Leonard increases communication far beyond what any typeset word could accomplish **(Fig. 3.A)**. The selected and collaged type styles are organized in a time line of style beginning with Egyptian hieroglyphics and ending with helvetica. This is made all the more clear by the horizontal rule that gives each of the type styles a common relationship and the type below the rule 1000 B.C. and 2000 A.D. Through these visual relationships much more is implied about the development and progress of humanity.

The informational posters by graduate design students from the Cranbrook Academy of Art deal with the problem of communicating a volume of information in a relatively small poster format. All three posters use conscious compositional strategies to guide the viewer from broad to specific information **(Figs. 3.B** through **3.D)**. The Jaugeon poster uses large images of geometric letterform construction and then color and line as a first level of communication to set the visual tone. By the time the viewer has visually digested this information and started to read the small specific information the subject matter is understood. The Celestial Navigation poster controls the space from foreground to background. The image of the sextant is closest to the viewer, and the perspective typography by sextant guides the viewer's eye back and forth from the title to the image and from the image to the title. The same foreground to background visual pull occurs with the line from sextant to moon to earth.

The Sutnar poster, designed by a graduate design student, is an informational poster about the design work of Ladislav Sutnar, a twentieth-century advocate of functional design **(Fig. 3.D)**. The variety and quantity of visual and verbal information in the poster requires strict compositional control. Color and placement first direct the viewer's eye to the title, then to the dimensional images that occupy the foreground. Subtitles are reversed out of black rules that guide the viewer to the blocks of text. The complex information is broken down into a series of manageable blocks of information to communicate on two levels: as a visual work that through images and organization describes the philosophy and practice of Ladislav Sutnar, and as a specific and detailed informational work through the information contained in the text.

3.C Katherine McCoy, instructor, Edward McDonald, designer, *Celestial Navigation* science information poster, Cranbrook Academy of Art, 1985.

3.D Katherine McCoy, instructor, Christopher Ozubko, designer, *Sutnar* typographic history poster, Cranbrook Academy of Art, 1981.

4.1 Silvestre, Nineteenth-century dimensional alphabet, ca.1843.

4.2 Wood-type alphabet, antique double outline shade, ca. nineteenth century.

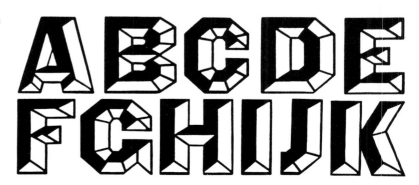

4.3 Wood-type alphabet, octagon, ca. nineteenth century.

Chapter 4
Three-dimensional Typography

Three-dimensional Typography

Three-dimensional typography in this chapter is defined as an identifiable volume, having length, breadth, and depth. This can be achieved by actually constructing the typography in three dimensions or by illustrating the letterforms with the suggestion of dimension. Both illustrated and constructed typography have an infinite number of viewpoints and angles of presentation from which the typography can be seen and represented.

Three-dimensional typography permits the letterform or word to become an object as well as a form of communication. On a two-dimensional surface, three-dimensional typography has the visual power of space and position and the potential of interaction with other objects in the compositional environment. Constructed three-dimensional typography can exist as both visual communication and sculpture in the environment.

The Historical Context: The Victorian Era

The eighty-two-year reign of Queen Victoria, from 1819 to 1901 was marked by prosperity brought about by the Industrial Revolution, as well as relative peace and security. The style of the period was one of excessively ornate decoration, and the subject matter was of saccharine, sweetness, and sentimentality represented by cherublike children, idealized maidens, and flowery motifs. The Victorian fondness for excesses of detail and decoration can also be seen in the intricately detailed gingerbread on houses, ornately carved wood of furnishings, and decorative style of many other manufactured goods. Graphic communications reflected this embellished style, and decorations of printers' ornaments, natural foliage, and ribbons, as well as highly ornate types styles, typify the period. In the stylistic bent of the period, which can be characterized as "more is more," it was thought that the letterform could enjoy a more expressive role through ornate detail and decoration and could be more influential in communication.

During this period printed materials became more easily available as literacy and commerce increased. In the new-found prosperity of the Industrial Revolution, a vast array of affordable goods were produced. The emerging working class became consumers of many more products than just the necessities of life. For the first time, manufacturers were faced with the problem of communicating to great numbers of people over large geographic distances. Competition among products and producers began and there was a need to attract the consumer's attention by means of broadsides, labels, boxes, and newspaper and magazine advertisements.

The style of the time can be characterized as eclectic, excessively ornate, and romantic. Value was a strongly perceived quality in the decoration, opulence, and intricacy that appeared on almost all printed surfaces and particularly on the packaging and advertisements of consumer goods. Manufacturers tried to outdo one another with outrageous claims of quality, miracle cures, and product performance. In visual communications these claims were expressed in the most ornate and lavish manner possible, with several embellished type styles and highly detailed engravings. The advent of modern advertising has its roots in this era, as does consumer skepticism.

Competition among producers was fierce, and owing to public demand, an entirely new vocabulary of display type styles was created (**Figs. 4.1** through **4.3**). Some

4.4 W. Baker & Co., cocoa advertisement, ca. nineteenth century.

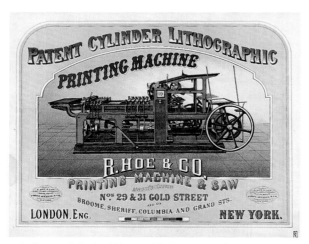

4.5 *Patent Cylinder Lithographic Printing Machine*, ca. 1870. Courtesy of the New York Historical Society, Bella C. Landauer Collection.

type styles mimicked the dimension of carving, with the addition of a shadow, outline, or decorative border. Other type styles became highly decorated with flowery tendrils or abstract patterns. It was felt that these type styles would more readily capture the viewer's attention and that the complexity would add to the perception of value.

In 1827 a method of mass producing wood type was developed with the process of lateral routing. These type styles of larger characters were much less cumbersome and less expensive than the metal characters were. Typical of the excesses of the Victorian Era, type styles that were exceptionally bold, large, decorative, and dimensional were created. Some of these communications resemble a visual battlefield in which dozens of elements vie for attention all at once.

In true Victorian fashion, an enormous variety of type styles were combined in visual communication broadsides and advertisements. The reasons for this were both stylistic and practical. The combination of many different type styles in a single work was a part of the decorative and overembellished style of the time. From a practical standpoint, display-size fonts of these decorative type styles were cut or cast and sold with only a limited number of characters. Frequently, there were often not enough characters of any one style to complete a job, especially text-heavy advertisements.

Characteristic of the time is the advertisement for Baker & Co. cocoa products **(Fig. 4.4)**. Eight different typefaces calling out eight different messages are used together with images of a highly detailed cornucopia of products and a heroic female figure. The communication value is diluted by the intense visual activity and number of messages being presented. The visual effect of opulence was far more important than was legibility.

Later in the nineteenth century, developments in the chromolithographic printing process enabled the efficient reproduction of more realistic and colorful images than ever before. In addition to the bold, bright, and saturated colors, subtle flesh tones, and minute detail—which before had been reserved for original oil paintings, this process permitted more accurate and realistic color representation and increased production in the printing process. The poster for the "Patent Cylinder Lithographic Printing Machine" features one of the new rotary lithographic presses that enabled printing production to increase more than five times that of flatbed presses **(Fig. 4.5)**. This improvement in production made the large-scale production of a daily newspaper possible. The poster is also typical of the design of the times. Ten typefaces are used to communicate the message and to illustrate some of the abilities of the press, with changes in tone, cast-and-drop shadows, and the accurate registration of color and images.

The first chromolithographic posters, such as the *Patent Cylinder Lithographic Printing Machine,* imitated the eclectic conglomeration of type styles from earlier broadsides. Gradually, with improved printing process, visual communication underwent a subtle shift from emphasizing the printed word to emphasizing the visual image. The amount of typography on posters was reduced in order to accommodate larger and more colorful images and to consolidate the verbal message to what was efficient, functional, and memorable. Because the quality of the printed image was so greatly improved, the typography became calmer, clearer, and more understated. Emphasis also shifted to unifying the composition elements—words and images—into a cohesive whole. Experiments with the abstraction of typography as well as imagery laid the visual groundwork for dramatic changes in graphic design.

Jules Chéret, whose work began to appear on the streets of Paris in the 1860s, is recognized as the initiator of the modern poster. He was classically trained at the Beaux-Arts in Paris while working as a lithographer's apprentice. He drew on the classical murals of the past for their ability to handle broad expanses of space, the visual language of folk art from circus posters, and his knowledge of the potential and limitations of the lithographic reproduction process.

Chéret was able to capture visually the mood of free-spirited effervescence in the figures in his work and therefore catch the attention and hearts of the public. The dynamic play of the figures and typography can readily be seen in *Les Girard* **(Fig. 4.6)**. The figures here are essentially a symmetrical series of intersecting angles. The bold use of black in the composition, unusual for the time, emphasizes the poster's dynamic angular quality.

4.6 Jules Chéret, *Les Girard*, 1879. Lithograph, 22⅝" x 17". Collection, Museum of Modern Art, New York, acquired by exchange.

4.7 Lucien Bernhard, *Osram AZO* poster, ca. 1910. Lithograph, 27 ⁵/₈" x 37 ³/₈".
Collection, Museum of Modern Art, New York, Purchase Fund.

Through the overlapping of forms, the active figures are bound to the typography, creating a unified composition. The typography is both treated as a flat, two-dimensional element and, through a play in illusory space, becomes three dimensional. This three dimensionality is much less obvious than the dimensioning or faceting of letterforms and exists because of the way in which the figures are intertwined with the typography, revealing foreground, midground, and background. One dancer's foot pierces the *o* in *L'Horloge*, and the dancer at the bottom moves in and out of the letterforms. The typography is drawn even more tightly into the composition because of its playful involvement with the figures.

The manner in which the figures interact with the typography in *Les Girard* is a departure for Chéret. Although his posters consistently reveal unified word and image compositions, *Les Girard* presents perhaps the most active and interesting involvement of the typography and figures. Other posters use dimensional letterforms created with traditional outline and shadowing techniques such as *Bal Valentino* (1869), *Moulin Rouge* (1889), and *Vin Mariani* (1894).

The Object Poster

After the turn of the century, new ways of approaching design, a result of the secessionist and Jugendstil movements, changed the face of the poster in Germany and Austria. More advertising oriented and commercial in nature, the poster was reduced to objective simplicity itself. Lucien Bernhard was one of the first to diverge from the style that Chéret had established and had made universally popular. Dubbing his work *Sach Plakat*—"object poster" or "fact poster"—Bernhard simplified the design of the product without embellishment and used flat color to convey strong visual messages.

The *Osram AZO* poster exemplifies Bernhard's strong and direct visual messages and is unusual in that the typography is given the suggestion of dimension **(Fig. 4.7)**. Some of the hallmarks of the object poster are its simplicity of type and image and flat color as in the *Priester* matches poster in 1905 and *Stiller* shoes poster in 1912. However, Bernhard is a master manipulator of color for maximum visual impact, as can be seen in the *Stiller* shoes poster, in which the black shoe illustration is emphasized by a bright red interior and an orange heel highlight. The *Osram AZO* poster consists of only the typography and product illustration, and its impact is unmistakable. The dimensional relief of the typography was a method of not only emphasizing the words but also of providing for the use of additional color to strengthen the impact further.

The development of the object poster presented a lasting form, style, and philosophy. Departing from the expressive and embellished work of the past, objectivity and function became the primary goals. Bernhard solidly reinforced this philosophy as the first professor of poster design at the Berlin Academy in 1920, and it was echoed even more loudly by the Bauhaus beginning in 1920. During this time and until the 1960s typography shed all qualities of expressionism in order to conform to the ideals of objective and rational communication.

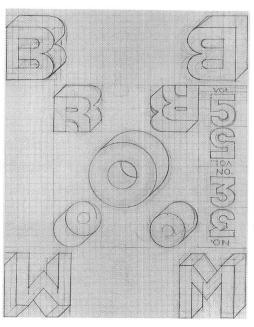

4.8 El Lissitzky, *Broom* magazine cover layouts, vol. 5, no. 3, 1922. Courtesy of the Van Abbemuseum, Eindhoven, Holland.

4.9 El Lissitzky, *Broom* magazine cover layouts, vol. 5, no. 3, 1922. Courtesy of the Van Abbemuseum, Eindhoven, Holland.

4.10 El Lissitzky, *Broom* magazine cover layouts, vol. 5, no. 3, 1922. Courtesy of the Van Abbemuseum, Eindhoven, Holland.

The Bauhaus

The examples of dimensional typography by Bauhaus designers Lissitzky and Schmidt are anomalies in the work being done at the Bauhaus in the 1920s and early 1930s. Most typographic compositions were based on the ideal of two-dimensional planar representation with sans serif letterforms. Function and communication of the message without embellishment of any kind were design dogma. The innovative later work of Schmidt in the early 1930s that began to explore new ways of using letterforms in photographic reproduction was interrupted and then cut short when the Bauhaus faculty was dispersed in 1932 and the school finally closed in 1933.

The three studies for a title page for the magazine *Broom* by El Lissitzky are rare examples of investigation into dimensional letterforms **(Figs. 4.8** through **4.10)**. Lissitzky, an architect, designer, and painter, was fascinated by the representation of dimensional space on the page. In deference to the prevailing goals of pure typography, particularly those of the Bauhaus, his letterforms, though dimensional, are simple, undecorated, functional sans serif. The movement of compositional space from dimensional to planar is intriguing in all three compositions, as is the obvious symmetry offset by the asymmetrical elements of the date, volume, and number of the issue. These works are studies that never enjoyed production.

Joost Schmidt, who succeeded Herbert Bayer as typography master at the Bauhaus in 1929, further developed this approach. Building less dogmatically on the doctrine of pure, functional, and rational typography established by his predecessors, Schmidt introduced new elements and a new way of compos-

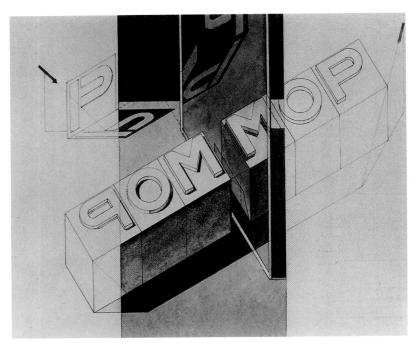

4.11 Joost Schmidt, The letters *MOP* in parallel perspective, in mirrored shadow construction, ca. 1930. Courtesy of the Bauhaus-Archiv, West Berlin.

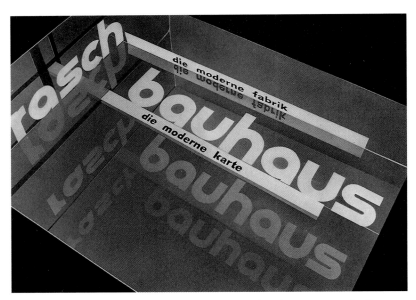

4.12 Joost Schmidt, *Bauhaus—the Moderncard*, cover of a prospectus by the wallpaper company Rasch Brothers & Co., 1930. Courtesy of the Bauhaus-Archiv, West Berlin.

ing typography. For the first time, photography and the commercial art studio were combined, and typographic elements were manipulated by actual reflection and transparency and recorded by the camera. The choice of reflective machine-age elements of the silver sphere (see Chapter 1, Figs. 1.3 and 1.4), the mirror in the parallel perspective study, *mop*, and the Plexiglas in the Rasch prospectus cover presented new compositional possibilities. The resulting compositions released typography from the flat planar presence from which it had been previously been pursued and investigated at the Bauhaus.

The *mop* study uses dimensional letterpress characters reflected in and through an illusory mirror surface **(Fig. 4.11)**. Both the *m* and *o* are symmetrical, and their reflection yields the same letters. An important visual clue to the reflection is the *p* that is obviously wrong reading on the left side of the composition. Without the *p* the viewer could confuse the sequence of the letters. Both the dimensionality and the reflective surface resulted in an unexpected and innovative composition.

The same qualities of innovation appear in the Rasch prospectus cover **(Fig. 4.12)**. The typography was composed on multiple Plexiglas planes and photographed. The resulting composition, initially composed of flat and planar typography and nonobjective elements of rules based on the Bauhaus philosophy, becomes three dimensional through repeated reflection. The use of modern materials and the photographic process made these works an innovative extension of the groundwork of Schmidt's predecessors. These insightful and experimental works never had a chance to mature fully and make as lasting an impact as did earlier works by Lissitzky, Moholy-Nagy, and Bayer, as they were created as the Bauhaus was being disrupted by the social changes in prewar Germany.

The Object Poster and the Bauhaus

The work on the object poster begun by Bernhard in Germany early in the twentieth century was strengthened and solidified by Baumberger and others in Switzerland beginning in 1919. Baumberger, who has been termed the spiritual father of the Swiss poster, embraced the qualities of the object or fact poster in his work and added technical expertise with the lithographic printing process (see Chapter 5, Fig. 5.13). In these works simplicity was supreme and decorative embellishment disappeared, leading to rational objectivity. The resurgence of the object poster coincided with the establishment of the Bauhaus. Here the ideals of the object poster and function were nurtured by and bound to the concepts of purified typography and visual structure as well as technology.

The resulting strength and pervasiveness of the Bauhaus philosophy of typographic objectivity cannot be overemphasized. Developed from earlier movements and strengthened by the consolidation of talent and public success, the Bauhaus's goal of typographic objectivity and rationalism precluded the investigation of embellishment. Typography took on a two-dimensional planar form and was relegated to the flat surface. Although experiments with image representation continued, the two-dimensional form of typography largely remained standard in compositions. It was also during this time that the role of the graphic designer became more defined and separated from the other visual arts. With the separation of art and design, typographic design became primarily a process of selection, placement, and structural control. Handcraft began to decline, and within a few decades the task of generating images fell mainly in the arena of other specialists, the illustrator and photographer.

Three-dimensional Typography in the 1930s

During the 1930s the philosophy of typographic objectivity was gaining momentum. Helmut Kurtz's *Neue Hauswirtschaft* poster and Otis Shepherd's *Wrigley's Spearmint Gum* poster are unusual for the time in that they employ three-dimensional typography. In both of these posters the three-dimensional typography is not used for decoration but for functional purposes.

The dimensional shadowing of the word NEUE is not done for embellishment in Helmut Kurtz's *Neue Hauswirtschaft* (new home economics) poster **(Fig. 4.13)**. Rather the dimensional shadow assists in visually organizing an active and complex surface. Photographs of an interior setting, dishes, pots and pans, and solid color areas compete for attention. The deep shadowing of the word NEUE acts as a visual starting point and organizes the composition for the viewer's eye. The letterforms are sans serif, and the dimensional shadowing provides a focal point in the composition.

4.13 Helmut Kurtz, *Neue Hauswirtschaft* poster, 1930. From the collection of Merrill C. Berman, New York City.

4.14 Otis Shepherd, *Wrigley's Spearmint Gum* poster, 1936. Lithograph, 42" x 28". Collection, Museum of Modern Art, New York, gift of the Wrigley Co.

Again, unusual for its time, Otis Shepherd's *Wrigley's Spearmint Gum* poster uses dimensional letterforms for the word *gum* (**Fig. 4.14**). The simplicity of the composition is in concert with the object poster's goal of simple and direct advertising which had been found to be both powerful in communicating messages and successful commercially. It is unusual that the word *gum* is given the visual prominence that had been reserved for words of connotative power, such as *war*. The letterforms jump off the page toward the viewer, and the visual force of dimension is combined with the psychologically unsettling diagonal composition. The image and the word bleed off two sides of the composition, visually enlarging the format. Finally, the simplicity of the poster consisting of only one word and the package front has a tremendous impact on the potential consumer.

Modern Three-dimensional Typography

The Bauhaus's goal of pure, functional typography has continued to be a powerful and persuasive force in graphic design. After World War II the object poster was further developed into what has become known as the international style. This resurgence was led by Swiss designers, many of whom had studied or taught at the Bauhaus, as well as designers from other countries who fled to Switzerland during the war. Swiss designer Josef Müller-Brockman, an initiator and leader of the movement, summarized its philosophy: "The principle which dominates over all others is typography without ornamental flourishes but whose form uniquely delivers the communication of the message."[1]

This philosophy of objective typography directed creative exploration in graphic design away from typography and toward image development and defined structures of organization. The expressive potential of typography was not emphasized until recently and so is largely unexplored. This philosophy was so dominant that examples of expressive typography from the 1930s through the 1950s are unusual enough to be called rare. Indeed, it was not until the 1960s and 1970s that experiments with three-dimensional expressive typography began to reappear in any number.

---

1. Müller-Brockman, quoted by Alain Weill, *The Poster, A Worldwide Survey and History*, Boston: G. K. Hall & Co., 1985, p. 311.

Dimensional typography in the nineteenth and early twentieth centuries was used to enhance communication by separating the typography from other elements, by visually pushing it forward on the compositional surface. This technique is still useful in modern communications, in that dimension has both a functional role in separation and an attention-attracting role, as the illusion of dimension is, by nature, an intriguing perceptual situation. Because typography in the modern context is most frequently flat and planar, dimensional typography also has become a novelty.

Perhaps one of the most interesting aspects of dimensional typography is its ability not only to improve communication but also to expand meaning. The posters by Milton Glaser, for example, *Dada and Surrealism* and *Concrete Poetry*, communicate much more than just the titles of exhibitions. They also give the viewer visual clues to the nature of the subjects and make a statement about each. Similarly, William Crutchfield's *Atlantis* and *Hope* compositions tell stories with one word, through dimensional typography placed in environments. In these works the expressive potential of typography begins to be realized.

Throughout his long and prolific career as a graphic designer, calligrapher, and typographer, Herb Lubalin was a visionary in developing typographic potential. He had a sensitivity to typography that enabled him to develop ideas for communications that were innovative and visually profound. Rather than arrange letterforms into ordinary and expected configurations, he developed new methods of treating letters and words as parts of a cohesive whole.

The two identities shown are similar and yet different in form. The *Dimension* identity is a single word, divided into three syllables and rendered so as to give the illusion of three sides of a cube **(Fig. 4.15)**. The word reads easily, even though the eye must travel from bottom to top, left to right, down and again left to right. The compressed letterforms and strong straight strokes enhance the x, y, z axes and the illusion of dimension. The *NBC, ABC, CBS* identity reads very differently **(Fig. 4.16)**. Here each set of three characters is intended to be an individual unit and reads that way, as well as being part of a cohesive whole at the same time.

4.15 Herb Lubalin, *Dimension* logo for the Radio Division of CBS, 1962.

4.16 Herb Lubalin, *NBC, ABC, CBS* logo, 1969.

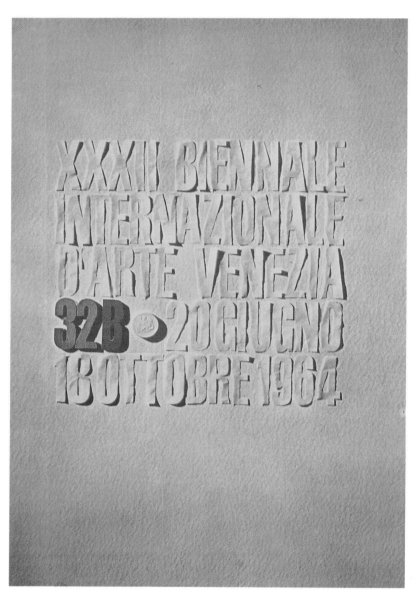

4.17 Massimo Vignelli, *XXXII Biennale* poster, 1964.

4.18 John Noneman, *Popular Optical Artball* poster for the Yale School of Art and Architecture, 1965.

Simple and symmetrical, Massimo Vignelli's *XXXII Biennale* poster broke new ground in typography **(Fig. 4.17)**. Rather than outlining, embossing, or setting the typography, the characters are cut out of paper. These flat paper shapes, in the same color as the background, are identified by the shadows created in the slight, irregular bending of the paper planes. Furthermore, the composition is photographed in much the same way that products would be, allowing the words to become the image. The symmetry is disturbed by the introduction of color and deeper shadow space of the "32B" and medallion. Although the poster is compositionally simple, the idea and realization are highly sophisticated and innovative.

Whereas Vignelli used photography to communicate dimensional type and shade and shadow, John Noneman used the actual dimensional qualities and properties of paper in his *Popular Optical Artball* poster **(Fig. 4.18)**. This poster, made with die cuts and scores, is a sculptural communication of typography and shadow. The typography is enhanced by communicating three times in three different ways: as printed characters, as dimensional characters, and as shadow characters. The poster overcomes the problem and expense of mail distribution, as it can be sent as a flat piece and folded upon receipt, thereby also involving the viewer as an active participant in the process.

4.20 Milton Glaser, *Concrete Poetry* poster, 1968.

4.19 Dorothe Hofmann, St. Clara's Church, inscribed sandstone floor, 1966.

The symbolic qualities of the timeless character of words inscribed into stone can be seen in Dorothe Hofman's work for St. Clara's Church **(Fig. 4.19)**. Cut into the sandstone floor, the words and symbols present themselves to the viewer upon entry. The Greek symbols for alpha and omega, the beginning and the end, symbolize the timelessness of the presence of God. The material used, stone, also relates to this timeless quality, with its ability to withstand weather and humanity.

Milton Glaser, a multitalented design visionary, has never been restricted by the prevailing design norms of the time. Rather, he approaches each design project with an open and creative mind. Glaser communicates clearly and eloquently in his choice and composition with illustrated dimensional letterforms. In his *Concrete Poetry* poster, Glaser visually expresses three definitions of the word *concrete*: (1) constituting an actual thing or instance, (2) an artificial stonelike material, and (3) concrete poetry—the fusion of visual form with poetic content **(Fig. 4.20)**. The word *poetry* lies closest to the planar surface, pierces the surface, and becomes the support for the plane and the word *concrete*. By designing the letterforms as dimensional characters, the meaning of the words are expanded in a way that the early twentieth-century concrete poets/designers did not envision.

4.21 Milton Glaser, *Dada and Surrealism* poster, 1968.

4.22 Chermayeff & Geismar Associates, sculpture for the Solow Building, 9 West 57th Street, New York City, 1974.

The *Dada and Surrealism* poster also expands its visual and verbal meaning **(Fig. 4.21)**. The table surfaces rest together, as do portions of the philosophies of the early twentieth-century art movements of Dada and surrealism. The Dada typography is pierced by the tabletop as a symbol of the negation of beauty and social order representative of the movement. The word *real* in surrealism is shadowed and isolated by the Dada table, thereby linking the purposeful irrationality of Dada with the subconscious dreams of surrealism. Finally, a larger table surface is suggested by the two table legs in the background, and the viewer is left to speculate on the typography that might exist on that surface.

In the midst of gray streets and sidewalks and the brick, concrete, and stone buildings of New York City sits a macroscale, bright orange, extrabold "*9*" **(Fig. 4.22)**. Designed by the well-known design firm of Chermayeff & Geismar Associates, this sign plays a dual role as city street sculpture and street number identification. As identification it can be spotted from blocks away, and as a sculpture people circulate around it as they pass or enter the building. The playful inventiveness of the sign makes it startling among the small wall-mounted and reserved brass and chrome numbers that appear on other buildings.

By profession William Crutchfield is a fine artist with a lifelong interest in the relationship of people to technology and its alluring pitfalls. Using wit and an observant and satirical eye, he frequently uses mechanical devices and machines as letterforms. The machines are mechanical contraptions consisting of cranks, gears, nuts, and bolts. The simplicity of the devices reveals a nostalgia for a time when people understood the machines they created and used. Perhaps the combination also shows a yearning for typographic communication

4.23 William Crutchfield, *ABC Crank-Up* watercolor, 1972.

before the complexities of modern life veiled the meaning and purpose of simple things. Finally, giving the letterforms a third dimension makes them expressive objects as well as words.

The experience the viewer brings to a work facilitates its message. The interpretation is open-ended and multilevel, through both the message's verbal meanings and the visual treatments Crutchfield employs. He uses a variety of two- and three-dimensional media and realizes his ideas in pen and ink, watercolor, prints, and wood and metal sculptures.

The *Alphabet Spire* series and *ABC Crank-Up* treat letterforms primarily as communication monuments **(Figs. 4.23, 4.24)**. Crutchfield considers letterforms to be inventions, and states, "My general notion concerning the Alphabet Series is that the letters of the alphabet are man's greatest invention."[2] The idea of invention is communicated through the crank handle on the bottom *A*. The letterforms are constructed so as to be both individual characters and elements connected to one another as a single unit. Transition is also a theme, with the letters emerging from one another.

The translation of two-dimensional graphic design into a three-dimensional surface is both a startlingly simple and a complex idea. The difficulties and variables of working on a flat surface are multiplied many times over in the consideration of environment, form, texture, and light.

2. Dorsky Galleries, Ltd., *William Crutchfield Watercolors, Prints and Sculpture*, New York: Dorsky Galleries, Ltd., 1973, p. 12.

4.24 William Crutchfield, *Alphabet Spire VI* laminated mahogany, 1974.

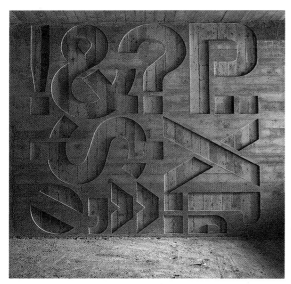

4.25 Armin Hofmann, Disentis School concrete wall relief, 1975.

What could have been just another concrete support surface becomes a playful sculpture of light and shadow when Armin Hofmann composed letterforms in cast concrete in the wall relief for the Disentis School in Switzerland **(Fig. 4.25)**. Punctuation marks, letterforms, and symbols all appropriate to the school environment are composed and cast in concrete. The meaning of these symbols is emphasized further because the surface is part of the wall and the wall is part of the building support system. The front surface of the wall uses a horizontal line grid made by the boards in the concrete mold. These horizontal lines are then contrasted with the curvilinear, vertical, and diagonal lines of the symbols and a vertical pattern of lines in the back planes.

Crutchfield's *Sea* watercolor shows water and movement in one word without illustrating either **(Fig. 4.26)**. Water and movement are implied by the word *sea* and by

4.26 William Crutchfield, *Sea* watercolor, 1975.

92

4.27 William Crutchfield, *Fly* watercolor, 1976.

4.28 William Crutchfield, *Fly* bronze, 1977.

the unlikely position of the letters on rocking chairs. The viewer mentally tips each rocking chair to provide movement that is occasionally synchronized and sometimes erratic but always moving, as is the motion of waves.

The word *FLY* actually begins to fly through the drawn illusion of movement and, in a later work, through the sculpted and cast illusion of form **(Figs. 4.27, 4.28).** Both the drawing and the sculpture show the same word when viewed from the other side, as the connecting planes fuse the word twice. This concept could be illustrated only by making the form transparent, as the double-sidedness of the form was difficult to interpret. It thus was natural for the artist to develop this idea in three dimensions.

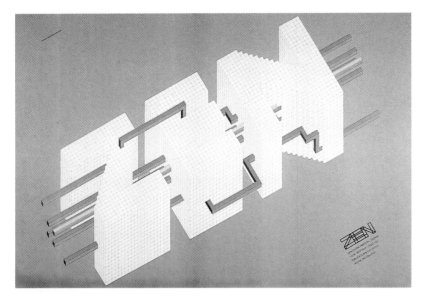

The *Zen* poster for the Zen Environmental Design group is a touchstone in the work of Takenobu Igarashi **(Fig. 4.29)**. By using dimensional letterforms, Igarashi was able to communicate visually a broad range of concepts by means of typography. The use of the dimensional word *Zen* empowers the self-contemplative attributes of the ancient Buddhist sect. This word also fuses the connotative meanings of Zen with the people and the work of the design firm. The dimensional typographic treatment also reflects the complexities of the design of three-dimensional space. The colored bars that connect the letterforms can be interpreted as the contemplative process of Zen.

4.29 Takenobu Igarashi, *Zen* poster, 1976.

4.30 William Crutchfield, *Atlantis* watercolor, 1977. Oil on Canvas, 58" x 35". Philadelphia Museum of Art, Louise and Walter Arensberg Collection.

4.31 William Crutchfield, *Hope* watercolor, 1977.

Complex ideas that ordinarily would require pages of words or a multitude of drawings to describe are communicated through the use of dimensional letterforms and simple environments in William Crutchfield's work. The mythical lost continent of *Atlantis* beneath the sea reveals only a nondescript portion of itself to the casual observer on the sea or from the air, but, beneath the sea, Atlantis remains intact, undiscovered, and waiting **(Fig. 4.30)**. *Hope* is constructed with the thinnest of threads tied to the smallest of rocks and teeters on its foundation **(Fig. 4.31)**. It may remain standing for a millennium, or a soft gust of wind may topple it at any moment. In Crutchfield's work, the viewer is an active participant, interpreting, speculating, and completing the scenario presented.

For the cover of the fiftieth anniversary issue of *Domus* magazine, Bob Noorda used typography as texture and communication **(Fig. 4.32)**. The gray background on the cover is a texture created by typography consisting of the names of the architects and designers who contributed to the magazine during its first fifty years. Overprinted on the gray typography is a dimensional "50," representing verbally the fifty-year span and visually the three-dimensional qualities of architecture. The planes of the "50" are also a colored texture so that the typographic background can be read. Noorda was able to achieve a broad range and scope of communication through his manipulation of texture, dimension, and meaning by means of typography.

4.32 Bob Noorda, Fiftieth anniversary cover of *Domus* magazine, 1978.

95

4.33 Milton Glaser, *Winter Festival* poster, 1981.

Milton Glaser's free-spirited *Winter Festival* poster shows dimensional letterforms as elements of the landscape **(Fig. 4.33)**. The words could be made of ice and set on a snowy hillside. Skiers move down the hill, around and about these objects, creating a random pattern of curvilinear ski trails. The illusion is heightened by the surfaces that reflect light and the shadows cast by the letterforms. By presenting the words as part of the environment, Glaser ties together the name of the event, the environment, the activities, and the people enjoying the festival.

Takenobu Igarashi's interest in the dimensional qualities of letterforms, as seen in his playful experimentation with three dimensions, has led to pragmatic yet innovative solutions to two- and three-dimensional design problems. Igarashi permits himself the joy of experimental investigation into dimensional typography simply for the fun of it. More abstract in meaning and yet more real in form than Crutchfield's typography set in environments, Igarashi's mirror alphabet series is, by its environmental context, both a sculptural investigation and a communication statement. The Mirror Alphabet *A* plays on the symmetry of some letterforms by completing the constructed half through a mirror reflection **(Fig. 4.34)**. Because the letterforms are actual constructed elements and not drawings dependent on illusion, the viewer enjoys a situation of reality of form and illusion of reflection. The mirror suspends, isolates, and places the letter *A* in the unlikely environment of a seashore. Just as the alphabet is an invention for symbolizing sound, the modeled dimensional *A* becomes a contrast of man-made object and idea within a natural environment.

Igarashi's interest in and investigation of dimensional typography led to his innovative applications in signing **(Fig. 4.35)**. The NN building sign brings the dimensional letterform to a macro scale. An exterior sign for a building, the *N* is repeated twice and can be viewed from all sides as the name of the building, *NN*. The grid tile surface gives texture to the massive form and breaks the surface into a series of squares and rectangles. The change in the shape of the tiles along the diagonal stroke gives the symmetrical forms an interesting asymmetrical texture. Specific signing for the tenants in the building is organized along the grid surface. This building sign has a dual purpose: As a communicator it identifies the building name and the locations of the tenants; however, it also is environmental sculpture to be enjoyed for its form, scale, color, and texture.

4.34 Takenobu Igarashi, *Mirror Alphabet "A"*, 1981.

4.35 Takenobu Igarashi, *NN Building* signing, 1981.

4.36 Takenobu Igarashi, *Plastic Alphabet II: K*, 1981.

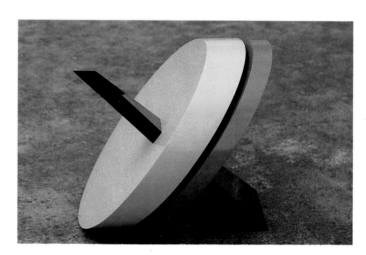

4.37 Takenobu Igarashi, *Plastic Alphabet II: Q*, 1981.

Exploring the qualities of material as well as environment, Igarashi created sculpture from typography with the materials of the industrial age. The *Plastic Alphabet* series works with the inherent qualities of plastic in terms of form and color **(Figs. 4.36, 4.37)**. The letterforms are geometric solid planes that intersect and occupy space. The *K* and *Q* can also be viewed as orthographic interpretations; that is, when viewed from a straight-on point of view, they appear to be traditional two-dimensional letterforms, but as the point of view is moved, a surprising and unexpected dimension is revealed. This work addresses the transplantation of the two-dimensional letterform into a three-dimensional environment and gives clues to the unseen dimensional potential.

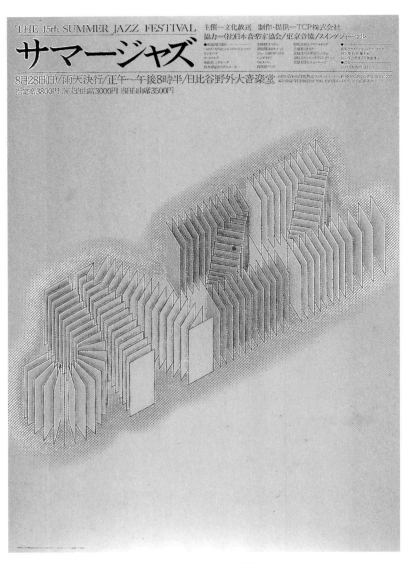

4.38 Takenobu Igarashi, *Summer Jazz* poster, 1983.

4.39 Takenobu Igarashi, *Igarashi* poster for the Atlanta Art Directors Club, 1984.

Igarashi's later two-dimensional work expands further his visual expression using dimensional letterforms and becomes even more sophisticated in illusion. His Summer *Jazz* poster uses a series of rhythmic planes to demonstrate the concept of multidimensional music **(Fig. 4.38)**. The *Igarashi* poster of 1984 introduces new elements to the dimensional type, including hand rendering, transparency, and optical illusion **(Fig. 4.39)**. The most recent of the works shown here, the poster for an Igarashi/Sato exhibition, uses die cutting and lamination to yield a three-dimensional surface **(Fig. 4.40)**. The selective peeling back of the grid surface reveals portions of the number 2 and a reflective surface. Igarashi's interest in three-dimensional typographic constructions is accompanied by an interest in drawn dimensional typography. The results from the three-dimensional constructed letterforms has inspired the two-dimensional investigations, and vice versa.

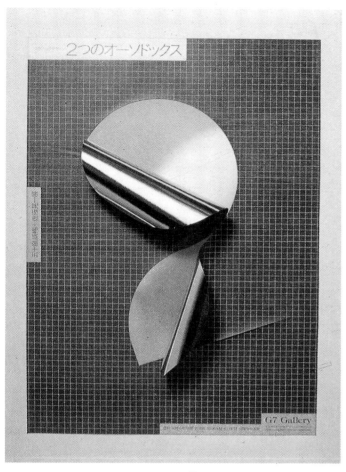

4.40 Takenobu Igarashi, *Igarashi/SATŌ Exhibition* poster, 1985.

4.41 Georganne Deen, *Oingo Boingo* record album cover, 1982.

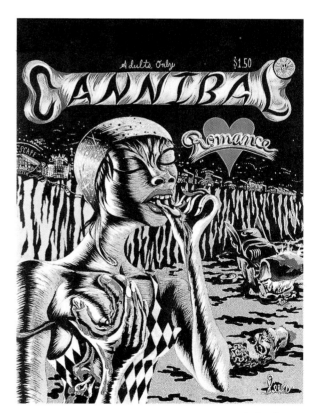

4.42 Georganne Deen, *Cannibal Romance* comic book cover, 1986.

Georganne Deen treats typography with the same attention and creativity she gives to her images. Her typographic style and approach have developed along with her images as an integral and important part of her compositions and never as an afterthought. Deen's expressive work centers on bold colors and startling and disturbing contrasts **(Figs. 4.41, 4.42)**. The cat figure in *Oingo Boingo* is humanlike in the manner in which it stands and is distinctly other-worldly with its sharp-toothed grimace and bulging eyes—in contrast with the delicate bow and bell on its tail. The typography is created with multicolored snakelike forms that contrast with the flat background space. These expressive contrasts also can be found in the *Cannibal Romance* comicbook cover. The planes of the figure are painfully stylized, uncomfortable forms, as is the variation in color. The typography has the same quality of haunting contrast.

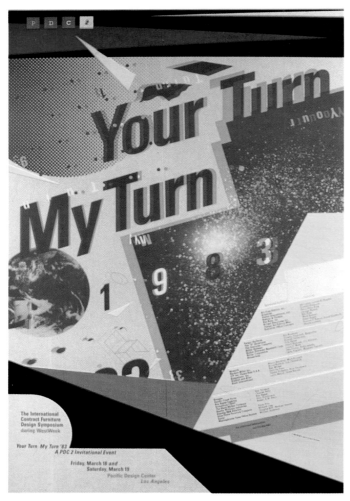

4.43 April Greiman and Jayme Odgers, *Your Turn, My Turn* poster, 1983.

4.44 Louise Fili, *Light* book jacket, 1984. (Painting by Claude Monet.)

4.45 J/J/R Creative Team Jung/Jung/Rodenhausen, Lucerne, Switzerland, *Polzer Wohnobjekte* card, 1985.

Using a method commercially developed in the 1950s and fleetingly popularized in 3-D movies, *Your Turn, My Turn* is one of a number of three-dimensional posters designed by April Greiman and Jayme Odgers **(Fig. 4.43)**. This method consists of off-register double printing tones of pale blue and red to yield an astoundingly realistic illusion of depth and dimension when 3-D glasses are worn. The full impact of the dynamic effect of typography floating in space amidst planes of varying depths and a night sky cannot be captured without 3-D glasses. (Placing a transparent red plastic film over one eye and a transparent blue film over the other eye can simulate the effect of 3-D glasses.) Nonetheless, the vibration of color, images, and type retains a large measure of its impact, no matter how it is viewed.

An implied light source creates letterforms by means of shadow on Louise Fili's *Light* book jacket **(Fig. 4.44)**. The letterforms are illusory and not drawn but are implied as dimensional via the gentle and beautiful cast shadows. Excessive letter spacing enhances the illusion and delicacy of the composition and allows the white background to flow through the composition. Even though the letterforms are not drawn, the visual implication raises them from the surface and creates the illusion of dimension.

The *Polzer Wohnobjekte* is a card for an industrial designer **(Fig. 4.45)**. The dimensional letterforms are highlighted by a spontaneous scribble that contradicts their precise construction. Further contrast is achieved with the small planar letterforms *MARTIN*. Each dimensional letterform presents a different angle of view in the same way that a dimensional product might be presented and the eye is reoriented with each new position in space.

The repetition of planes and movement enhance the *Graphis* magazine cover by Rosmarie Tissi **(Fig. 4.46)**. The letters are transparent figures attached to a grid surface. The outline of the transparent type contrasts with the fine red outline. The planes and letterforms are arranged on a curve that moves down the page as the planes turn and tilt in space.

Fred Troller used pattern to disrupt visual space and shadow to create the illusion of dimension **(Fig. 4.47)**. The surface of the design is constructed with a regular horizontal line pattern. By slightly jogging the line pattern as it meets the letters, the characters appear to be bent out from the flat surface. The addition of a light source and bold shadows strengthens the recognizability of the letters. The illusion is both delightful and convincing.

4.46 Rosmarie Tissi, *Graphis 241* cover, 1986.

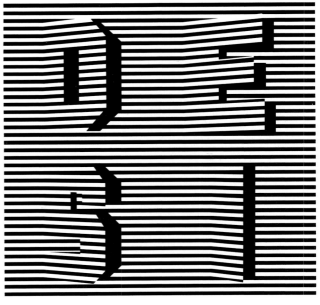

4.47 Fred Troller, *DESI Award* identity, 1986.

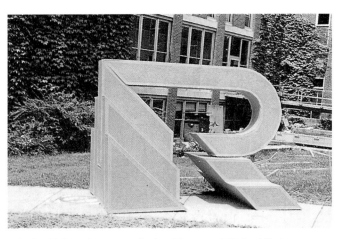

4.A David Svet, instructor, Carlos Rivero and Elaine Wyder, designers, Typographic form study, *R*, The Ohio State University, Department of Industrial Design, 1987.

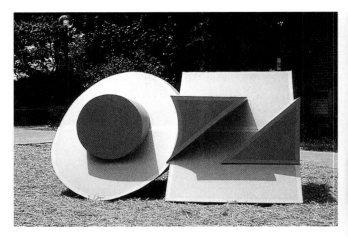

4.B David Svet, instructor, Lori Sherman and Robyn Long, designers, Typographic form study, *OZ*, The Ohio State University, Department of Industrial Design, 1987.

4.C David Svet, instructor, Steve Andriano and Sharon Bryant, designers, Typographic form study, *Q*, The Ohio State University, Department of Industrial Design, 1987.

In the basic design courses he teaches, David Svet uses architectural-scale three-dimensional letterforms for the investigation of scale, structure, light, and shadow **(Figs. 4.A** through **4.C)**. Letterforms were chosen for this exercise because of their known orientation, structure, and symbolic value as visual signs, which allow experimentation with three-dimensional forms while retaining their legibility.

The students, working in teams, made thumbnail sketches, drawings, and a series of small sketch models before constructing a final large-scale model. The final architectural-scale models were produced from inexpensive and easily handled four-feet-by-eight-feet corrugated cardboard sheets. The finale for the project was held in an outdoor courtyard with the exterior environment as a backdrop and the sun as a light source.

The students discovered that creative exploration of letterforms' dimensional qualities also had to consider legibility. This was the case as well in proportioning the structure, as the proportions of the letterforms were found to be critical to both aesthetic and functional considerations. Finally, light, shadow, and multipoint viewing revealed some of the sculptural aspects of dimensional typographic design.

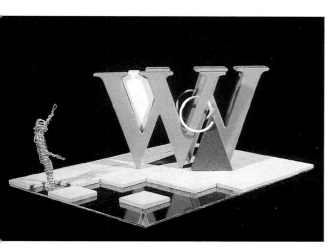

4.D Kimberly Elam, instructor, Jan Ostendorf, designer, *WOW*
Worlds of Wonder signing, The Ohio State University, Department
of Industrial Design, 1988.

In the advanced visual communication design course at The
Ohio State University's Department of Industrial Design, students developed a three-dimensional free-standing sign for a
toy manufacturer, Worlds of Wonder, using the initials WOW
(**Figs. 4.D** through **4.F**). The objectives of the project were to
investigate the potential of letterforms as both three-dimensional communication elements and street sculpture. A toy
company was chosen for this project, as it presented many
interesting visual possibilities of form, color, and texture.

The initial sketches were very two-sided, almost as if the
typography had been extruded and placed upright. By rapidly
moving from sketches to sketch models, the project's dimensional and sculptural qualities became apparent and presented
many additional visual possibilities. Research into modern
materials and methods of construction inspired solutions rang-
ing from inscribed and inset sidewalk areas to the use of clear
plastics and reflecting pools. The final solutions to the project
indicate some of the visually powerful possibilities of dimensional typography.

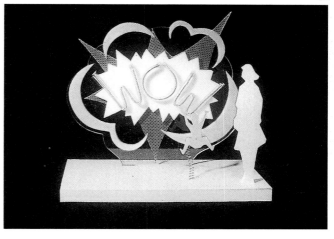

4.E Kimberly Elam, instructor, Molly Kestner, designer, *WOW*
Worlds of Wonder signing, The Ohio State University, Department
of Industrial Design, 1988.

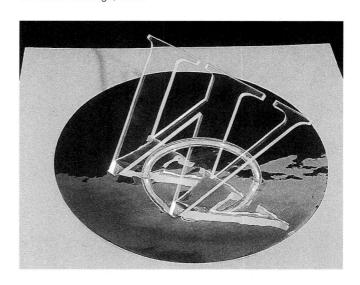

4.F Kimberly Elam, instructor, James Molloy, designer, *WOW*
Worlds of Wonder signing, The Ohio State University, Department
of Industrial Design, 1988.

103

4.G Kimberly Elam, instructor, David Bennett, designer, Typographic composition, *Memphis*, The Ohio State University, Department of Industrial Design, 1985.

4.H Kimberly Elam, instructor, David Bennett, designer, Typographic composition, *Memphis*, The Ohio State University, Department of Industrial Design, 1985.

The experimental investigation of dimensional typography is part of an intermediate typography course **(Figs. 4.G** through **4.J)**. The purpose of this exercise is to give the student designers an opportunity to investigate creatively typography as dimensional elements. The word *Memphis* was chosen because of the well-known furniture and accessory design of the Memphis group. The Memphis designs, employing playful combinations of solid geometric forms, bright colors, textures, and patterns, were used as inspiration.

The first *Memphis* composition, by David Bennett, was done in black, white, and gray tones. This approach encouraged a focus on the development of dimensional

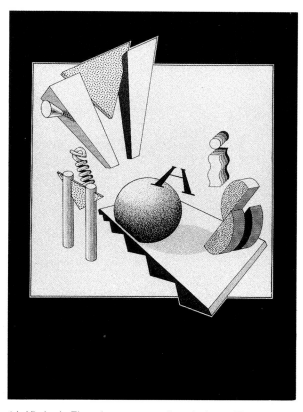

4.I Kimberly Elam, instructor, student designer, Typographic composition *Memphis*, The Ohio State University, Department of Industrial Design, 1985.

4.J Kimberly Elam, instructor, student designer, Typographic composition *Memphis*, The Ohio State University, Department of Industrial Design, 1985.

letterforms and the composition of those elements in the format. The dimensional letterforms are difficult at first to visualize because they are so contrary to previous experience. After the black-and-white composition is finished, the students use it as a base for a color composition. The consideration of color opens up another new set of variables as color enhances both depth and the three-dimensional character of the letterforms. Color also alters the manner in which the composition is viewed, and so that it can be manipulated to enhance eye flow or meaning.

5.1 Geoffroy Tory, Alphabet from *Champ Fleury*, 1529.

5.2 Silvestre, Human figure alphabet, ca. 1843.

5.3 J. Midolle, Gothique composée alphabet, ca. 1834.

5.4 J. Midolle, Alphabet diabolique, ca. 1834.

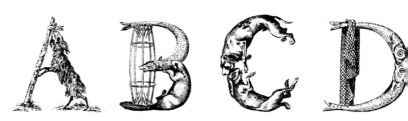

5.5 Silvestre, Nineteenth-century French animal alphabet, ca. 1843.

5.6 Silvestre, Nineteenth-century French tree alphabet, ca. 1843.

Chapter 5
Iconographic Typography

Iconographic Typography

Iconographic typography refers to typography that is also a pictorial representation of a natural or man-made object. Through creation by illustration, photography, or sculpture, the typography has a resemblance or is analogous to an identifiable object, plant, animal, or person. The combination of typography and iconography yields a visual and verbal message of direct obvious meaning with the possibility of many additional implied meanings.

The Historical Context: The Victorian Era

The creation of type styles, with the letterforms consisting of iconographic representations, can be seen as essentially a nineteenth-century, Victorian invention (see Chapter 4). However, an earlier example, from 1526 can be found in the *Champ Fleury*, by Geoffroy Tory **(Fig. 5.1)**. This alphabet is created with tools representing the letter shapes of the alphabet. Although it is one of the first printed indications that letterform construction can extend pictorially beyond symbolic representation, Geoffroy Tory guides his readers to Egyptian hieroglyphics for still earlier examples.

During this period designers were not content to treat letters as merely abstract symbols for sound and so responded with a plethora of decorated and embellished typefaces **(Figs. 5.2** through **5.4)**. The intent of these highly stylized, sometimes dimensional, and often conglomerated type styles was to emphasize the meaning and importance of a visual message by means of detail and decoration. In addition, the competition for the attention of consumers and clients in the midst of a communication explosion forced artists and designers to include unusual novelties in their work. Type foundries also competed fiercely for business. Often type styles were created from human figures, gothic cathedral architecture, and even devils, to serve as novelty advertisements for type foundries and printers or to promote a particular type designer.

Some Victorian type designers, taking clues from the decorative initials of medieval manuscripts and printed matter, developed type styles in which each letter was an initial capital composed of objects rather than using a traditional frame as a foil for imagery **(Figs. 5.5, 5.6)**. These alphabets were display faces used primarily to advertise the creativity, quality, and attention to detail, offered by a printer, designer, or foundry. Such letters were used more to attract attention than to convey a message.

Technology

Victorian iconographic type styles were carved by hand and then cast in metal. The fonts of object types were then sold to printers and distributed. The attention to detail and the complexity of the type styles made them a technological and trade craft tour de force. Accordingly, they were very expensive and were rarely offered

5.7 Edward Penfield, *Harper's* July cover, 1894. Zinc etching, 18" x 12½".
Collection, Museum of Modern Art, New York, Exchange.

in more than one size, which immediately limited their use. As novelties, these type styles usually offered only capital letters, as they were mainly used as initial caps that would offset a body of text, and as display type for single words. The complexity of the forms made them unsuitable for lowercase letters and the obvious problems of legibility precluded extensive use.

Cast metal letterforms and carved or routed wood types were used in the printing process of letterpress, in which raised surface characters were assembled in a matrix, locked up, inked, and printed by pressure. Letterpress printing was used exclusively to print books and other text-heavy materials. Images printed by the letterpress method were limited by the lockup matrix and needed to be engraved in wood or metal before they could be reproduced. By the late nineteenth century, however, broadsides and posters were increasingly printed by lithography, because the image and type could be drawn on a flat stone surface, thereby allowing the artist more creative freedom and the possibility of more detail in the representation of the image. This process further encouraged the development of type and image compositions by a single artist, thus assisting in the unification of type and image compositions. As the popularity and quality of chromolithography grew, fewer metal types were used to produce popular large-scale posters.

Art Nouveau

By the beginning of the art nouveau period in 1890, chromolithography was producing images of incredible detail, quality, and subtlety of tone (see Chapter 6). The visual image of the poster became larger, free from square or rectangular boundaries, and vivid in color. The combination of the art nouveau style and vastly improved technology helped improve and unify the compositional qualities of the poster. The scale of the poster and its popular appeal of colorful images on drab city streets encouraged a shift in visual emphasis from type to image. This transition prompted the development of typography as a pictorial object and image.

In 1894, in the midst of the art nouveau movement, typography was drawn and shaped by hand to enhance the illustration and composition, and letters were also created by combinations of images and typography. For example, Edward Penfield used firecrackers to create the typography for the July cover of *Harper's* magazine **(Fig. 5.7)**. The image and typography are bound to each other by the tension of the lit match as it nears the fuse of the firecrackers, and the viewer's eye and mind automatically complete the expected sequence. Penfield's composition has a definite backround, midground, and foreground. The firecracker letterforms in the foreground are the most important element; behind them is the figure; and finally, behind the figure is the magazine's masthead.

Alphonse Mucha used all of the technology of his time to create his *Gismonda* poster **(Fig. 5.8)**. Using the classical imagery of a Byzantine mosaic, a life-sized scale, and rich vibrant colors, the poster was an overnight sensation that launched his illustrious career. Created, printed, and distributed in less than a week, the poster delighted its subject, actress Sarah Bernhardt, who gave Mucha a six-year exclusive contract to design her theatrical posters.

The typography in *Gismonda* is made up of mosaics that give the letterforms a natural abstracted stylization of the process of cutting and fitting small tiles. The typography is not a separate element but is integrated into the poster. The use of the architectural background gives the figure a classically heroic setting and provides a surface for the typography.

In Belgium, art nouveau in the 1890s was celebrated by artists through dramatic and colorful posters that lined the city streets. The fine arts community was thriving with cultural groups and publications, and Brussels became one of the poster capitals. Artists such as Privat-Livemont, Ferdinand Toussaint, Weiluc, and Victor Mignot brought innovative illustrations and typography to both the posters and the city streets.

5.8 Alphonse Mucha, *Gismonda* poster, 1894. Museum Vleeshuis, Antwerp, Belgium.

5.9 Ferdinand Toussaint, *Café Jacqmotte*, ca. 1896. Museum
Vleeshuis, Antwerp, Belgium.

5.10 Weiluc (pseudonym of Lucien-Henri Weil), *Frou-Frou*, 1900.
Museum Vleeshuis, Antwerp Belgium.

The changing social climate can be seen in the female figures in
Toussant's and Weiluc's posters **(Figs. 5.9, 5.10)**. Toussaint's
woman is an idealized and classic, romantic figure, ageless
feminine, and sensuous yet aloof and untouchable. But in Weiluc's
Frou-Frou poster the female figure is young, beautiful, and
naughty. She shows her legs and, as further proof of her
liberation, she is smoking a cigarette.

In Toussant's poster *Café Jacqmotte* the flowing lines and lush
colors are typical of art nouveau. The stylization extends to the
typography which is created out of the steam rising from the coffee
cup. The typographic illustration indicates that this work was
created near the height of art nouveau, as the undulating forms
initially reserved for the female figure, flora, and decoration are
also used for the typography. In *Frou-Frou,* the typography is
created from the smoke of the cigarette, lending an air of mystery
and an ephemeral quality to the composition. In each work, the
artist fully integrates the typography with the visual image by
combining the smoke or steam with the letterforms and also
attracts the viewer's attention through the novelty of the pictorial
typography.

5.11 Julius Gipkins, *Kaiser Brikett* poster, 1913 (Berlin).

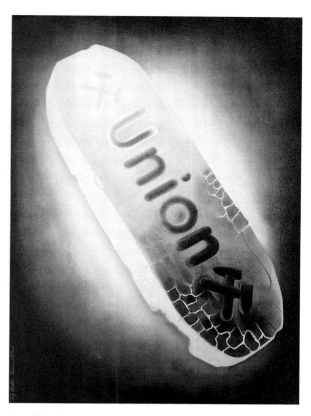

5.12 Fritz Bühler, Poster for a brand of coal (Plakat für eine Kohlenmarke), 1943. Courtesy of Gewerbemuseum Basel/Museum für Gestaltung, Poster Collection.

The Object Poster

There is a dramatic difference between how typography as an object is treated in art nouveau and later in the twentieth century. During the art nouveau period, typography is a fanciful stylization of the obvious illusions of steam, smoke, mosaic tiles, and the like. Indeed, the intention of the art nouveau artist was to blend color, romance, and image into a graceful and unified composition. The communication of the subject matter is less important than the aesthetics of beautiful illustrations of women and highly stylized typography. Later typographic treatments, particularly those in the 1920s, are strongly tempered by reality and functionalism. By that time, the idealized female figure was regarded as unreal and unnecessary decoration for the conveyance of a message and so disappeared. Decorative typography and pictorial typography also disappeared, remaining only in the context of reality and verbal functionalism. The new philosophy was called *Sach Plakat*, or object poster, and used a simplified design of the product and typography that is both precise and unemotional.

Both Julius Gipkins's *Kaiser Brikett* poster and Fritz Bühler's poster for coal briquettes exemplify the object poster, with the image of each being a simple portrayal of the product being advertised, coal briquettes **(Figs. 5.11, 5.12)**. The compositions are similar in that the product fills the poster format, and the typography in both exists only as it does in reality, embossed on the briquette during production.

The style and intent of both posters also are similar. Gipkins was probably influenced by some of the object poster's originators, including Lucien Bernhard, whose impact was first felt in 1905. Bühler was probably influenced by Baumberger and other contemporaries who revived and renewed the object poster beginning in 1919. Later, the Bauhaus developed and altered the object poster according to its philosophy.

Technology is responsible for essentially the same poster appearing in two different forms. In 1910, when Gipkins designed his poster, the reproduction of full-color photographic images was a new technology, and chromolithography was far more popular. He thus relied on his own skills to produce an illustration symbolizing glowing heat. But by 1943 the process of color separation for full-color printing had been popularized as well as perfected, and Bühler was able to photograph and reproduce a red-hot, glowing coal.

5.13 Otto Baumberger, *PKZ* poster, 1923. Photo courtesy of the Reinhold-Brown Gallery, New York City.

The *PKZ* poster was done while Otto Baumberger was a professor of lithography and drawing at the Applied Arts School of Zurich, Switzerland **(Fig. 5.13)**. As an educator and a practicing professional, Baumberger was well aware of the dramatic changes occurring in graphic design. Between the end of art nouveau in 1910 and 1923, when the *PKZ* poster was created, the movements of cubism, collage, futurism, suprematism, de Stijl, and constructivism all had touched graphic design. Baumberger devised a philosophy and a style regarding the function of words and images that became a catalyst for a new visual language.

In the poster for PKZ, a manufacturer of men's clothing, communication is reduced to the simplest elements possible. A tweed coat is laid open and fills the poster format. An embroidered label provides the only typography, "Marque PKZ." Rather than show the entire coat, which would detract from the message by emphasizing one particular style, the compositional window zooms in on a portion of the coat, causing the viewer to focus on the quality of fabric and attention to detail in the garment. The communication is then expanded as the viewer immediately relates the ideas of good fabric and detailing to all of the other clothing in the PKZ line.

The composition is enlarged and completed in the viewer's mind, owing to the way in which the coat bleeds off all four edges of the poster. The lines created by the edges of the coat, lining, and lapel could allow the viewer's eye to leave the format. But instead, the button in the lower right corner provides a visual resting place and an opportunity for the eye to return to the upper portion of the poster, the PKZ label.

Baumberger achieves compositional unity of type and image in a manner similar to that of the art nouveau designers, but his purpose was very different. The typography of the PKZ label is a reflection of reality and not an illusionary concoction. The illustration of the garment is realistically rendered as well and is enhanced only by the use of a cropped format. The object poster and the philosophy of functionalism were echoed by other designers and by the Bauhaus, becoming a powerful and lasting force in graphic design.

Walter Kach developed the idea of the object poster very differently in his *Form Without Ornament* poster **(Fig. 5.14)**. The hammer and pliers are illustrated entirely with typography which at the same time also communicates verbally. The typographic elements function in a dual role as verbal and visual communicators. The rigid horizontal/vertical configuration of the hammer is con-

112

5.14 Walter Kach, *Form Without Ornament* exhibition poster, 1927. Courtesy of the Museum für Gestaltung, Zürich.

5.15 Georg Trump, *Bielefeld* poster, 1927. From the collection of Merrill C. Berman, New York City.

trasted by the diagonal/curvilinear form of the pliers. Tension is created at the top of the hammer and the left edge of the pliers near the edge of the format while movement is created as the right edge of the pliers bleeds off the bottom of the page. Kach thereby compared the functional role of typography with the function of other manufactured tools, by making the words become the image.

By the 1920s, photography had become a new medium of experimentation for designers, and its undisputable documentary ability made it ideal for the object poster. Georg Trump's *Bielefeld* poster was designed for an exhibition at the Bielefeld School of Applied Arts, which taught printing and typesetting **(Fig. 5.15)**. Similar to Baumberger's *PKZ* poster, Trump's image focuses only on the elements necessary for maximum, direct communication. Instead of approaching reality with a realistically illustrated and lithographed image, however, the essence of the image "object" is captured with photography. The designer thus ceases to be an artist in the traditional role of handcraft and instead becomes a developer of concept and execution with photography and typography.

5.16 George Krikorian, *New York Times Crossword Puzzle* poster, 1950. Offset lithograph, 45" x 58". Collection, Museum of Modern Art, New York, gift of The New York Times.

5.17 Herb Lubalin, *Rock and Roll*, 1957.

5.18 Seymour Chwast, *Elektra Productions* moving announcement, ca. 1965.

The image consists only of a hand holding a composing stick, a tool used to produce letterpress printing, and the metal type in the composing stick is the name of the town, Bielefeld. All unnecessary image elements have been eliminated. The remaining elements therefore yield much more in connotative communication than the obvious communication of the hand and the composing stick, a combination that allows the viewer to complete, as part of the message, the images of location, people, and letterpress printing.

Modern Iconographic Typography

Many of the current examples of iconographic typography have the same purpose as did the first object posters. The current intention is to communicate directly and powerfully with the most precise means possible, that is, creating words as images by means of iconographic typography. The combination relies on the verbal communication qualities of typography and expands them with pictorial treatment. The resulting works convey a specific message and also evoke connotative images.

George Krikorian designed the image of the crossword puzzle to become its own advertisement **(Fig. 5.16)**. Using the poster format, he drew a crossword puzzle grid, with the message of the advertisement in the horizontal and vertical words. He used positive and negative space to organize as well as place the type, and color to organize the message. The background is red, which attracts attention, and "The New York Times" is reversed white on black to draw attention to the newspaper's name. The other type is black on white, and all the type is drawn in handwritten print to complete the connection with the crossword puzzle.

Herb Lubalin has been a typographic innovator throughout his career. He brought to typography a skilled hand, humorous insight, and a keen eye unbound by popular convention. Using typography as a vehicle for communication he has merged objects with words to make both humorous and thought-provoking statements. In *Rock and Roll* the copy reads: "Ever since rock was a stone and a roll was a bun . . ." **(Fig. 5.17)**. The typeset *o*'s are replaced with a rock and a roll. The composition is controlled in terms of the elements' order of importance to draw the viewer to the piece and through the complete message. First noticed are the words *rock* and *roll*, then the objects that replaced the *o*'s, and finally the complete text.

The Elektra Productions' moving announcement is as delightful as some of the fanciful art nouveau types **(Fig. 5.18)**. Each of the eclectic typographic characters has its own means of mobility, from wheels to feet to shoes. The characters march and roll across the card to their new location. Coupling the name of the company with mobility, Seymour Chwast emphasizes both in the specific verbal and visual aspect.

In the FDR book cover Chwast again combined the image and type in order to enhance communication **(Fig. 5.19)**. This design solution relies on the viewer's previous knowledge of the meaning of the symbols used. The well known silhouette of Franklin Delano Roosevelt doubles as the *D* in the initials. The initials are a form of shorthand for the lengthy full name, and the silhouette reinforces this shorthand with a concise visual/verbal

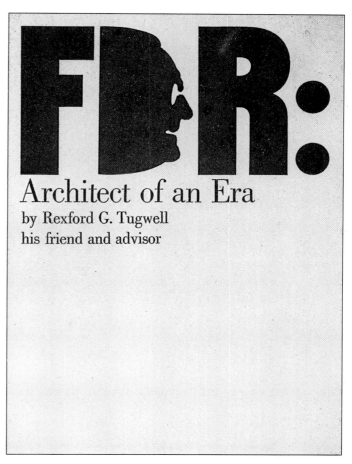

5.19 Seymour Chwast, *FDR* book cover, 1968.

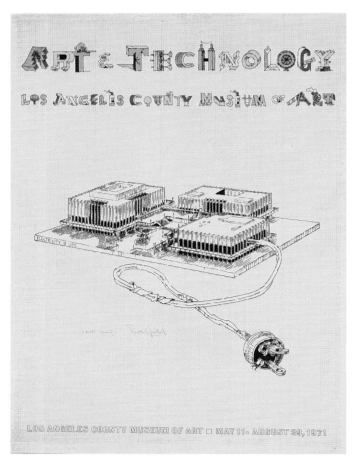

5.20 William Crutchfield, *Art & Technology* poster for the Los Angeles County Museum of Art, 1971.

5.21 William Crutchfield, *I Remember Technology* poster, 1971.

combination. Most of the message is packed into the initial-and-silhouette combination that is emphasized by its placement and bold construction and is consequently understood at a glance. The subordinated and more specific information is in smaller, lighter-weight letters.

Dimensional illuminated typography has been a continuing theme in William Crutchfield's work (see Chapter 4). Crutchfield views typography and machines as vehicles to convey deeper meanings. The *Art and Technology* poster for the Los Angeles County Museum of Art is drawn on engineering grid paper **(Fig. 5.20)**. Each of the letterforms is a part of an invention. The curious irregularities in the illustrations remind the viewer that all inventions, including typography and technology, are manufactured. A final statement is made in the electrical cord and plug that extend from the museum building, which alludes to the fact that buildings are also a technology of questionable nature.

The same is true in the *I Remember Technology* work **(Fig. 5.21)**. The sphere that dots the *i* has obviously and

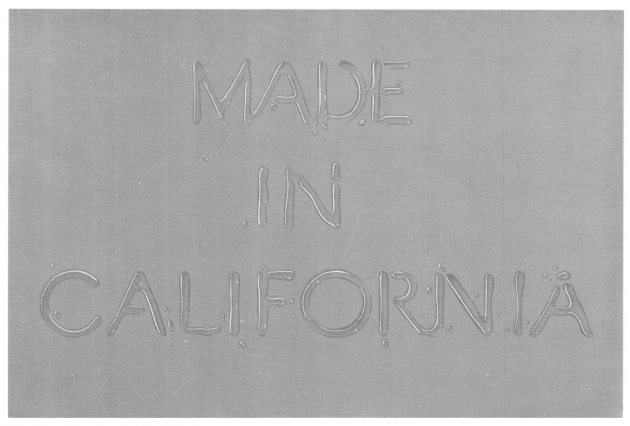

5.22 Edward Ruscha, *Made in California* typography, 1971.

rather precariously been placed there by someone who climbed the ladder leaning against the column. There is a sense of nostalgia in the inventions that are represented by the letters, as they all recall a time when technology was or seemed to be more understandable. The letters, as well as the wheel, tunnel, rudder, hinge, and I-beam, all are easily understood inventions that, in this electronic age, have become more complex and less readily understandable.

Edward Ruscha's *Made in California* typography is another combination of both language and image **(Fig. 5.22)**. It is interesting to compare the connotative qualities of black type set on a white background with Ruscha's expressive work **(Fig. 5.23)**. The typeset words offer few, if any, images to the viewer. Any connotations are cold, impassioned, and lifeless. Ruscha's typography is drawn so as to give the illusion of being made with water and is intensified with a vivid orange color. The viewer draws on connotative qualities of water/California/color to conjure up images of the sea, sunshine, and oranges.

MADE IN CALIFORNIA

5.23 *Made in California* typography (comparison).

5.24 Alexander Calder, *Calder's Circus* poster, 1972. Offset lithograph, 36" x 27¹/₂". Collection, Museum of Modern Art, New York, gift of Peter Stone.

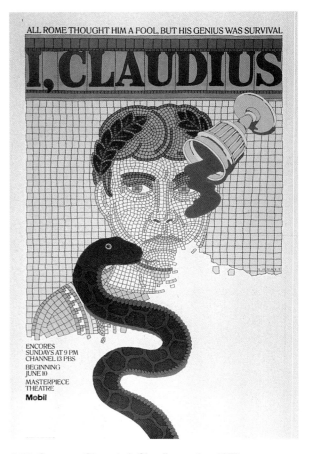

ALL ROME THOUGHT HIM A FOOL, BUT HIS GENIUS WAS SURVIVAL

I, CLAUDIUS

ENCORES
SUNDAYS AT 9 PM
CHANNEL 13 PBS
BEGINNING
JUNE 10
MASTERPIECE
THEATRE
Mobil

5.25 Seymour Chwast, *I, Claudius* poster, 1976.

Alexander Calder used the same playful sculpted wire to create typography as he did to create the figures of his *Circus* poster and his mobiles **(Fig. 5.24)**. In the poster, the wire acts as a drawn line of starts, stops, and tensions in the representation of objects, people, and typography. The line gains dimension, thereby giving an illustration space and volume. The acrobat hangs precariously from a hook, and the angle of the body and the flow of the hair recall the kinetic qualities of Calder's work. The typography is composed with the same care, from a single piece of neonlike wire bent to form the typographic characters that flow from the acrobat's hands. The slight radius of the baseline adds to the sense of the figure's swaying movement, even in the poster's two-dimensional form.

The illusion of ancient mosaics are used as the image, and the tiles are used as typography, in Seymour Chwast's *I, Claudius* poster **(Fig. 5.25)**. The mosaic typography here is vaguely reminiscent of Mucha's mosaic typography in his *Gismonda* poster made almost one hundred years earlier. The styles and purpose of the

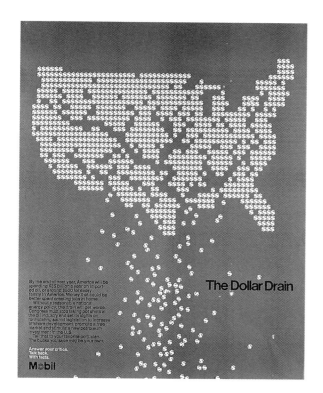

5.26 Bruce Blackburn, *Mobil Dollar Drain* poster, ca. 1978.

5.27 Bruce Blackburn, *Mobil Gasoline Market* poster, 1978.

two posters are different, but both use the historic reference to classical tiles and ancient mosaics. Both posters also were made for dramatic productions: *Gismonda* for a Sarah Bernhardt play and *I, Claudius* for a Masterpiece Theatre production. The style of the *I, Claudius* poster is highly graphic, uses flat color, and is more complex and revealing in composition. *I, Claudius* uses the setting as historic reference and reveals much more about the deception and intrigue in the production (murder by poisoned wine and venomous snake bite).

Bruce Blackburn's *Dollar Drain* and *Gasoline Market* posters use images created with the texture and symbolism of type **(Figs. 5.26, 5.27)**. The *Dollar Drain* poster uses dollar sign symbols to form a map of the United States, and the *Gasoline Market* poster lists the names of independent oil companies in red, white, and blue, forming the American flag. In these posters the type is far more than just texture; it combines verbal and symbolic visual meaning to create a powerful image and statement. In the *Dollar Drain* poster, the dollar signs flow through the map and out of the country. In the *Gasoline Market* poster, the names of hundreds of independent oil companies indicate the business structure of the country. The major theme of each poster is clearly and rapidly communicated through the type and image combinations, which amplify the message.

5.28 Herb Lubalin, *It Takes All Types* advertisement, 1978.

5.29 Herb Lubalin, *How to Become Successful Though an Art Director* series, 1979.

5.30 Herb Lubalin, *How to Become Successful Though an Art Director* series, 1979.

Herb Lubalin interprets, revises, and updates Silvestre's *Human Alphabet* of the nineteenth century to the twentieth century, to suit his particular message. In *It Takes All Types* Lubalin uses a play on words to combine typography with all types of different people **(Fig. 5.28)**. The message, for an advertising studio, is that there are no standard solutions to individual clients' needs. Each letterform is fancifully drawn as a distinctly different person and personality. The verbal message and visual humor are clear.

In his *How to Become Successful Though an Art Director* series **(Figs. 5.29 through 5.32)**, Herb Lubalin invites the reader to do what he has done in his work: "Open your eyes. Look around. Perceive. Observe. Expand your viewpoint. And above all, recognize the significance of an 'O'." The replacement

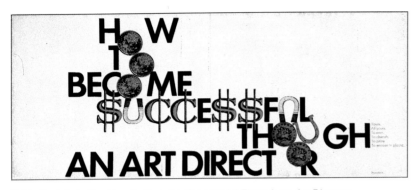

5.31 Herb Lubalin, *How to Become Successful Though an Art Director* series, 1979.

5.33 Herb Lubalin, *Spasm* advertisement, 1979.

5.32 Herb Lubalin, *How to Become Successful Though an Art Director* series, 1979.

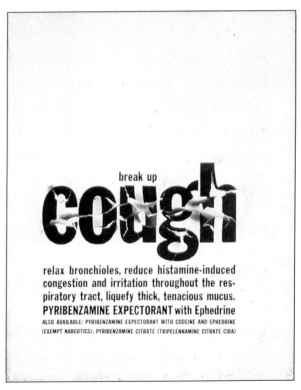

5.34 Herb Lubalin, *Cough* advertisement, 1979.

of the *o* in these works allows each piece to carry a different visual message, although the major verbal message is the same. Lubalin uses symbols and pictorial imagery for vision, money, luck, men and women, the globe, and the bagel.

Lubalin's *Spasm* and *Cough* advertisements portray the ailments through object and typography combinations (**Figs. 5.33, 5.34**). The "S" slinky configuration in the word *Spasm* depicts the tension and compression in muscle spasms. The spontaneously torn paper in the *Cough* advertisement clearly relates to the uncontrolled force of a cough. In both ads the viewer completes the designer's image by visualizing the cough that tore the paper or the kinked muscle in the spasm.

121

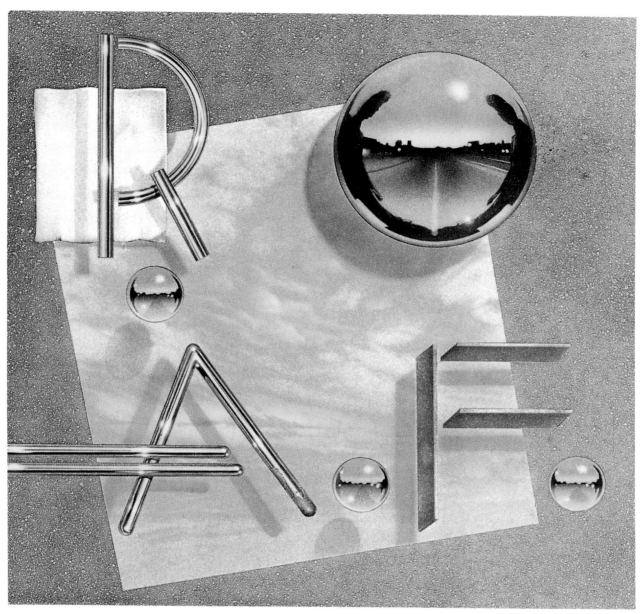

5.35 Charles White III, *RAF* album cover for A & M Records, 1981.

Charles White III is a master of the illustrated illusion and collage composition. His deft use of tone, texture, and form creates letterforms from chrome tubing and rectilinear planes **(Fig. 5.35)**. Glass spheres reflect people, and objects are juxtaposed with a cloud-filled sky. The illusions are realistic and intriguingly composed to keep the viewer guessing as to whether the sky is, indeed, dimensional space or is an illustrated panel containing the shadows of the letters. The periods of the initials RAF are small, marblelike repetitions of the large sphere that guide the viewer's eye through the composition. The composition is a new interpretation of meaning for a music group that hints, with chrome and sky, at the traditional meaning of RAF, Royal Air Force.

Christopher Hopkins also uses the sky as a backdrop for a collage of objects **(Fig. 5.36)**. Again, the viewer is uncertain as to whether the sky represents space or is a backdrop for the objects' shadows. Two different light sources increase the visual ambiguity. The unlikely combination of a cigarette butt, smoke, marbles, and a stencil number, along with their shadows, forms the 1982 New Year message. The border rules intensify the feeling of a compositional window and space.

The semantic qualities of the license plate typography of Kit Hinrichs's *AIGA California Design* poster portray the legendary symbolism of the car in California **(Fig. 5.37)**. With more cars per capita and more miles of highway than anywhere else in the world, the car is, indeed, representative of the state. The vanity plate, or custom license plate, is popular in California, as are clubs for vintage car enthusiasts. The license plate and an *AIGA* bumper sticker hold all of the necessary verbal information. The combination of a concise verbal message and an expansive visual message makes this a memorable statement.

5.36 Christopher Hopkins, *1982* poster for Margarethe Hubauer, 1982.

5.37 Kit Hinrichs, *AIGA California Design* poster, 1982.

123

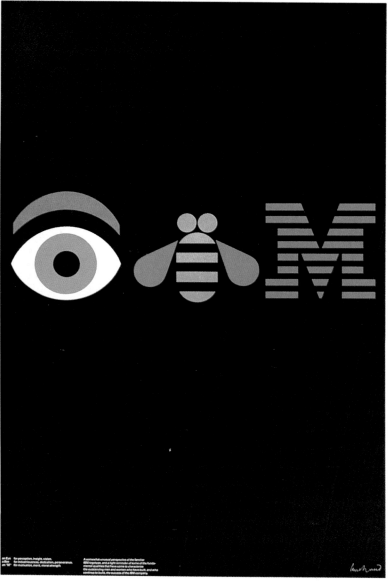

5.38 Paul Rand, *IBM* poster, 1982.

The rebus quality of Paul Rand's *IBM* poster is visually delightful and intriguing, especially because it is for IBM, one of the world's leading high-tech companies **(Fig. 5.38)**. The replacement of the letters with images underscores the message in an unexpected way. The image of the eye conveys not only the importance of vision but also the sense of the company's visionary planning and development of products and services. The bee has long been a symbol of highly organized industriousness which is one of IBM's qualities. This poster is startling in that one would expect visual images of chrome and circuit-board intricacy to represent the complex technologies of IBM, but the unexpected simple and traditional symbols seem to say much more.

John Weber chose a plastic template as the vehicle for expressing the identity for *Long's Commercial Art Supply* **(Fig. 5.39)**. The letterforms are geometric shapes die cut from the traditional "eye ease" green template plastic. These shapes together become the name Long's. Form, color, and configuration all relate to the template and its connotative relationship to the professions that use them. The small, printed message at the bottom of the template gives the address and telephone number. Appropriateness in combination with humor and novelty make the identity unique.

The December 1980 cover for *U&lc* features Stan Brod's unique holiday message **(Fig. 5.40)**. The Hebrew letters for *shalom* (peace) are stylized into the shape of a dove to become a dual word-and-image greeting. The characters are formed out of the graceful and fluid shapes of a bird in flight which are enhanced by the contrast of thick and thin. The dove appears ready to fly off the page, owing to the tension created by the edge relationships of the dove's tail and head to the format edges. The symbolism of the dove of peace and the word *shalom* announce a universal message.

The animated forms of the dancers' bodies make dynamic letterforms for Steff Geissbuhler's *Alvin Ailey Dancers Twenty-fifth Anniversary* poster **(Fig. 5.41)**. The letters are composed of dancers' silhouettes captured in flight as they leap off the floor. Each letter emphasizes the control, elegance, and grace of the human form. A single dancer is used for both the *v* in Alvin and the *a* in Ailey, by placing the arms in the first word and the legs in the second; the leotard acts as negative space, separating the two letters and portions of the body. The substitution of dancers for letters combines denotative and connotative meaning in a concise and expressive message.

5.39 John Weber, *Longs Commercial Art Supply* identity, 1983.

5.40 Stan Brod, *Shalom* cover for *U&lc*, 1980.

5.41 Steff Geissbuhler, *Alvin Ailey Dancers Twenty-fifth Anniversary* poster, 1985.

125

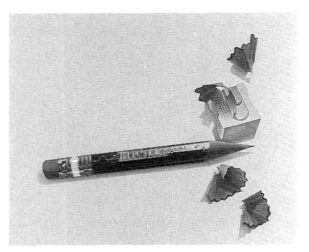

5.42 Barbara Banthein, *TeleChoice* illustration, 1986.
TeleChoice is a registered trademark of U.S. WEST.

5.43 Michael Schwab, *Susan Crutcher* letterhead and card, 1986.

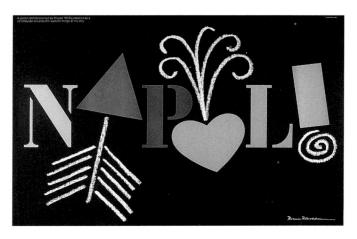

5.44 Bruce Blackburn, *Napoli* poster, 1986.

The visual image of the pencil has many connotations. Pencil writing is easily revised and erased any number of times. Pencils are inexpensive and found almost everywhere. Barbara Banthein gathered together these semantic qualities of the pencil and the name of a new product service into an advertisement for "TeleChoice" **(Fig. 5.42)**. The combination of the visual image and the typography communicates visually what would take paragraphs to explain verbally.

Fanciful forms become typographic characters in Michael Schwab's letterhead for a film editor **(Fig. 5.43)**. Illusory changes in space are indicated by a texture pattern and the presence of a light source. The letters are recognizable objects such as a snake, magnet, and pyramid as well as abstract dimensional configurations of the *s* and *n*. Such forms are suitable for a film editor, whose stock and trade is illusion.

The substitution of objects for letters can expand the meaning of a word or the meaning associated with a city, as in Bruce Blackburn's *Napoli* poster **(Fig. 5.44)**. The substitution of the arrow pointing up for the *a* signifies achievement, present and future, and the substitution of the heart and fountainlike lines for the *o* are symbolic of an outpouring of caring and compassion. The exclamation point that takes the place of the *i* indicates excitement. The stencil type indicates a human hand and the people. Together, the symbols and letters express a range of desirable qualities for a city.

Nocturne is a regional Arizona magazine of art, entertainment, music, and dining, as indicated by the symbols along the right edge of Jim Cherry's cover **(Fig. 5.45)**. This cover is for the premier issue and is subtitled "Nocturne looks with optimism toward the new year." The rope-and-wood letters combine with the other characters in an eclectic fashion to become an identity and to hint at the magazine's diversity of subjects.

5.45 Jim Cherry III, *Nocturne* magazine cover, 1987.

5.46 Woody Pirtle, *AIGA* poster, 1987.

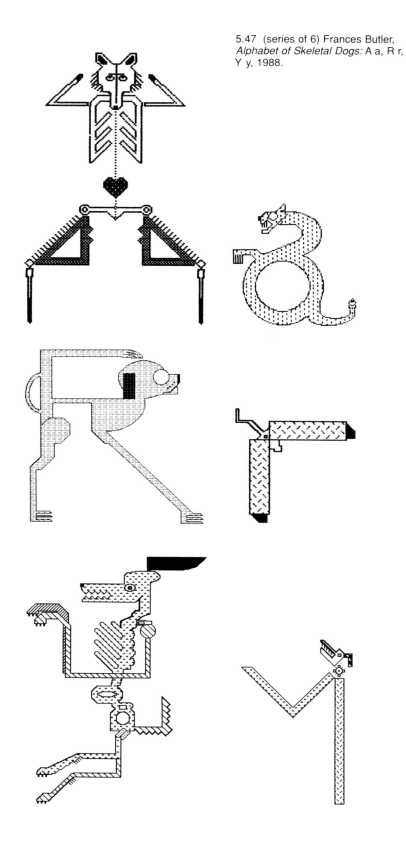

Woody Pirtle selected and collaged objects and typography for maximum effect and impact **(Fig. 5.46)**. In his *AIGA* poster for the first annual design conference in Boston, he chose a teapot for the city that hosted the first "tea party" that led to the American Revolution. To update the symbol, tea bag tags—a modern invention—hang out of the teapot with images and names of the various designers who attended the conference. The images and typography are expressive of the range of people, locations, and subjects that will be represented at the conference.

Frances Butler experimented with letterforms and images in her *Alphabet of Skeletal Dogs* **(Figs. 5.47)**. She used a Macintosh computer to bind together the images and typographic characters. The flat space occupied by the figure is reminiscent of Egyptian hiero-glyphics—their symbolic value as well as decorative style. The pixelated character of the imagewriter output device gives the fig-ures an alien feeling and a sense of the shapes' systemization. In many ways the computer has encouraged designers to re-examine the past and to create new realities with inspiration from the old.

128

5.A (series of 2) David Svet, instructor, Gregory Bonnell-Kangas, designer, visual substitution project, The Ohio State University, Department of Industrial Design, 1988.

Visual substitution was used as a theme in an exercise for intermediate level graphic design students **(Fig. 5.A, 5.B)**. An imaginary signing project was constructed for a supermarket. Students were asked to develop a sign series for a product area of the store that would expand on meaning and communication by substituting visual images for typographic elements.

The students were limited to hand-graphic techniques. Visual representation through illustration is difficult, for the objects must be clearly communicated through the drawing. The main problem was selecting unusual objects for representation, such as choosing an orange peel instead of an orange.The students also tended to make the signs too involved, which inhibited rather than facilitated communication. Students discovered that there were many ways to depict an object and that the best way was often the most obvious choice.

5.B (series of 3) David Svet, instructor, Angela M. Canini, designer, visual substitution project, The Ohio State University, Department of Industrial Design, 1988.

6.1 Jules Chéret, *Palais de Glace*, 1896.
Courtesy of Museum Vleeshuis, Antwerp,
Belgium.

Chapter 6
Abstracted Typography

Abstracted Typography

Abstracted typography uses characteristic letterforms shapes but alters them by nonrepresentational means such as line, plane, and color. This definition is broad and indeed could include much of the work in this book. In this chapter, however, abstracted typography is limited to typography that has retained its flat, frontal view and single-plane orientation, is clearly related to traditional set type, and has been transformed and acquired visual connotations through nonrepresentational means.

The Historical Context: Technology

It is impossible to ignore the sweeping changes that technology has brought to art and design. For example, the invention of photography changed the way that artists approached their work. Photography diminished the need and desire for art to simulate reality in the visual recording of people, events, and objects, and because photography was able to capture reality so well artists could not compete. Accordingly, the concept of recording reality shifted to interpretating reality. This new idea of translating the subject matter in art welcomed innovation and abstraction.

The use of foundry type in posters was eclipsed by improvements in the lithographic printing process, whereby the artist drew directly on the stone printing surface. Because type was drawn rather than selected from the wood or metal fonts on hand, the typography could be made compatible with the imagery as in Chéret's *Palais de Glace* (**Fig 6.1**). In addition, the freedom of the lithographic process permitted the typography to be placed anywhere on the page, to follow curves, to flow with the image, or to occupy foreground, midground, or background space. Both the fluid forms of the art nouveau style and the technology of the chromolithographic process encouraged the abstraction of typography.

Art Nouveau

Abstracted typography originated in many of the fine arts and design movements and technological developments of the late nineteenth and early twentieth centuries. But because this was a period of such rapid change, it is exceedingly difficult even to mention all of these varied influences. We shall therefore discuss only art nouveau, de Stijl, constructivism, expressionism, and purism, in order to simplify the complexity of visual evidence regarding abstracted typography.

Some of the roots of abstracted typography can be found in the art nouveau movement. Art nouveau, in turn, grew out of the earlier arts and crafts movement in response to the industrial age, and it encompassed all of the visual arts: painting, architecture, industrial design, and graphic design. The many terms for this movement varied by region: *art nouveau* was used in the United States and Britain, *secession* in Austria, *jugendstil* in Germany, and *le style moderne* in France. Each of the names for the movement is coupled with the term *new* or *young*, as the

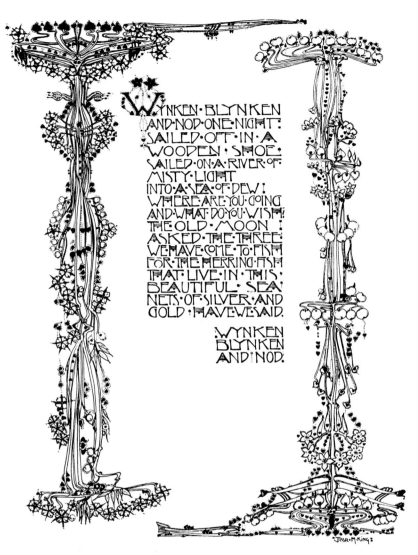

6.2 Jessie M. King, *The Studio Page*, Wynken Blynken and Nod, 1899.

6.3 Marjorie Rhodes, *art nouveau alphabet*, 1900.

movement emphasized innovation. Although this move ment, consisting of many variations on a theme, antici pated future developments, it also contained references to and influences of the past.

Many influences can be cited as inspiring the art nou veau movement and its development. In addition to the arts and crafts movement, Japanese woodblock prints were circulating in Europe by the 1880s and became, by the 1890s, the height of fashion for artists and collectors alike. These prints demonstrated the visual power of closure, silhouette, flat color, and positive and negative space, and simplified the graphic translation of natural forms. The subjects of these prints were from both everyday life as well as more extraordinary occurrences. European artists were readily able to transfer these forms and subject matters to posters, with innovative designs and profitable results. Painters and printmakers the graphic designers of the time, welcomed the oppor tunity to expand their craft beyond paintings or prints and to popularize it through the poster.

Jules Chéret was a master of combining the qualities of the mural, the fine arts, and the translation of his subjects into the popular idiom. One of his creations is the image of a beautiful, carefree, fashionable young woman who became known as "La Chérette," as seen in his *Palais de Glace*. Note that in this poster the typography is drawn with the same hand and fluid style as is the image: The restrictions and limitations of metal type no longer apply, and the type is placed on a curved baseline to give it the same elegant style as the image has. During the art nouveau period typography became fully integrated into posters as compositional elements, as seen in Chéret's placement of "Champs-Elysées" in the background, the figures in midground, and "Palais de Glace" in the foreground.

By the height of the art nouveau movement, near the turn of the century, the transition from innovation with images to innovation with typography was complete. Chromo lithography technology provided the newest means for typography to be as unconventional and abstract as the image was. This can be seen in Toussaint's *Café Jacqmotte* poster (see Chapter 5), in which the elegance of the swirling curvilinear line extends to and is empha sized in the typography. The typography, in turn, extends from and with the image as a result of the steam rising from the coffee cup.

Just as lithography permitted the free-flowing line of stylized imagery released from the labors and restrictions of engraving, it also provided more expressive means for typography. In Jesse M. King's *The Studio Page*, the typography is based on a hand-drawn system of repetitive proportions and strokes **(Fig. 6.2)**. Because the characters are drawn individually, they can be made to fit the justified column and the aesthetic sense of the designer. The characters are expanded to fill short lines and are condensed and tucked in to one another on long lines—a method impossible with metal letterpress characters. The result is a typographic composition as lyrical as the nursery rhyme inscribed on it.

Although chromolithography and the hand stylization of type was particularly well suited to the art nouveau poster, there remained a multitude of printing works that could be inexpensively produced by letterpress methods. To meet the needs and desires of the time, art nouveau typefaces were designed and cut or cast specifically for the letterpress market **(Figs. 6.3, 6.4)**. From simple to ornate, these types brought the art nouveau style to scores of printed materials, including magazines, newspapers, broadsides, advertisements, and books.

Secession

The secession movement was started in 1898 in Vienna by a group of dissident artists and architects from the Fine Arts Academy led by Gustav Klimt and including the Group of Seven architects led by Josef Hoffmann and Otto Olbrich. This group was able to bring vitality and innovation to the decorative arts by challenging and redefining the traditional hierarchy of art. Initially influenced by the allegorical symbolism of the arts and crafts movement, the secessionists rapidly developed a more simplified and abstract design style. Later, this style continued to evolve through the Wiener Werkstätte (Viennese Workshop), under the direction of Josef Hoffman and Koloman Moser, until 1932, and through the Deutscher Werkbund, established in 1907, which eventually led to the establishment of the Bauhaus.

The sucession movement spoke publicly and eloquently through its publication *Ver Sacrum* (Rite of Spring), exhibits, and posters. From 1898 to 1903 *Ver Sacrum* featured the work of the masters and initiators Koloman Moser, Alfred Roller, Josef Hoffman, and many others.

6.4 Art nouveau alphabets, ca.1900.

133

6.5 Alfred Roller, *XIV Secession*, 1902. From the collection of Merrill C. Berman, New York City.

6.6 Alfred Roller, *XVI Secession*, 1902. From the collection of Merrill C. Berman, New York City.

6.7 Designer unknown, *1. Ausstellung der Jury Freien* poster, ca. 1905. From the collection of Merrill C. Berman, New York City.

In the work of Alfred Roller and that of many other secessionists, controlled experimentation with abstraction and pattern was not limited to representational imagery. Rather, the typography became an element of abstracted texture in much the same way that the textural images did. In Roller's poster *XIV Secession* the letters are formed from heavy strokes of curves, lines, and angles, a texture that is reflected also in the patterns of the image **(Fig. 6.5)**. By the time the later *XVI Secession* poster was designed, the letterforms were still more abstracted, with the counters stylized, curved, and compressed as the representational imagery was eliminated and the typographic texture became the image for the poster **(Fig. 6.6)**.

These compositions are balanced and harmonious in comparision with the asymmetry of art nouveau in general. The style and form of these posters can be directly connected to the Glasgow School of Art and the work of Charles Rennie Makintosh which had been exhibited at secessionist exhibitions in 1900 and 1902 and became an overnight sensation.

The *1. Ausstellung der Jury Freien* (First Exhibition Without Jury) poster was made 'or an exhibition in the city of Brünn, then in the Austriar Empire but now Brno, Czechoslovakia **(Fig. 6.7)**. The avant-garde keynote of the exhibition was assured, in that the works were not of subjective jury selection. It is also visually expressed in the abstracted design of the poster. The type is again a texture of very black sans serif abstracted typography, whose function is subordinated to the abstract texture and form. The composition and typography reflect the architectonic structures of secessionism as well as the typographic proportions, vertical stress, and high center strokes of the Glasgow school.

De Stijl and Constructivism

From the abstracted imagery and typography of art nouveau and its many variations and innovations developed a visual investigation into a new structural order. Early twentieth-century experiments yielded a new visual language of abstracted pictorial form in painting and the fine arts. This new language was translated into design by the movements of de Stijl and constructivism.

In about 1917 de Stijl was conceived as a purifying force directed toward typography that eliminated decorative elements such as serifs and advocated the pure function

6.8 Fritz Schleifer, *Bauhaus Ausstellung* poster, 1923. Photo courtesy of the Reinhold-Brown Gallery, New York City.

of communication. Typographic letterforms and images were composed of a series of simple horizontal and vertical rectangles or squares, and compositions were restricted to the use of primary colors and black. The later constructivist principles of the 1920s were similar in regard to the functional role of typography. The movement also embraced a communist ideology that advocated good design for society at large and not just an elite.

Schleifer's *Bauhaus Ausstellung* poster reflects influences of both de Stijl and constructivism **(Fig. 6.8)**. The abstracted geometric head of the figure and letterforms use the rectangular elements of letterpress rules and markers. According to the philosophies of these two movements, the materials used in the industrial reproduction process represent honesty and purity. The selection of color is limited to the primaries, and red was chosen for the "eye" of the figure as it competes effectively with black for visual attention. Simple, direct, and highly abstract, this work embodies the Bauhaus principles of functionalism and unity with technology.

Expressionism

The expressionist movement began in the late nineteenth century and continued well into the twentieth century. It enunciated a powerful visual statement reflecting the artist's or designer's intense personal emotion. Artists such as Vincent van Gogh and Edvard Munch gave the movement legitimacy, with their bold colors and psychic deformations. Popular street art such as the poster followed with the knowledge of the dramatic impact of such images.

The development of the expressionist movement in the twentieth century paralleled the development of the motion picture in the 1920s, and consequently many film posters show its influence. Germany's economic collapse after World War I left the nation impoverished and without goods to sell or money to buy them. In this depressed economic climate, often the only work for poster artists was posters for the increasingly popular cinema.

One poster of this period that exemplifies the elements of expressionism is the Schulz-Neudamm poster for Fritz Lang's *Metropolis* **(Fig. 6.9)**. There is a jarring emotional contrast in the angles and planes and in the use of shade and shadow. The cityscape and typography contrast with the curvilinear lines and planes in the robot figure, with the typography exemplifying these contrasts in the use of only straight lines to form curvilinear characters. The vertical strokes of the typography become elongated, obtuse triangles that appear to pierce the city as they descend. In all, the poster offers an expressionistic and morbidly intriguing glimpse of the future.

Purism

The purist movement advocated rigorous compositional order and the precise treatment of objects and materials. In many of the posters of this movement, both the typography and the imagery are created by hand, but none of the visible signs of brush strokes or irregularities remains. The ultimate control of tools, production, and printing are brought to bear in removing the poster from the expressive illustrations of the past. These posters can be viewed as the visual mechanizations of design, imagery, and typography, and their compositions are based on the classic principles of proportioning, such as the golden section. The work of A. M. Cassandre shows innovative methods for focusing on and depicting such imagery.

These purist influences extend directly to the typography, which Cassandre felt played an essential role in the poster: "It's the star of the wall stage because it alone is charged with telling the public the magic formula that sells. The poster artist should always begin with the text, and set it, as far as possible, in the center of the composition. The design should be based on the text and not inversely. "[1]

1. Cassandre, quoted by Alain Weill, *The Poster, A Worldwide Survey and History*, Boston: G. K. Hall & Co., 1985, p. 200.

6.9 Schulz-Neudamm, *Metropolis* film poster, 1926. Lithograph, 83" x 36 1/2". Collection, Museum of Modern Art, New York, gift of Universum-Film Aktiengesellschaft.

6.10 A. M. Cassandre, *Étoile du Nord* poster, 1927. From the collection of Merrill C. Berman, New York City.

The purist influences of order and precision are reflected in A. M. Cassandre's posters *Étoile du Nord* and *L. M. S. Bestway* **(Figs. 6.10, 6.11)** The compositions contain meticulously controlled proportions, geometric elements, and interrelationships of form. Their restrained, stylized, and technically perfect style is indicative of the movement's love of and faith in the technology of the industrial age.

The order and precision of these posters extend to their abstracted typography. In *Étoile du Nord* the precise geometry of the letterforms is softened by a dot tone texture. The relationship of the awkward width of the *o* to the other letterforms is reduced with overlapping and transparency. Subordinate type marches around the perimeter of the poster, framing the compositional window. Cassandre's use of all caps makes the words look like compositional blocks of abstract texture as well as elements of verbal communication. As in many of Cassandre's posters, the circle is an element of importance and compositional control. The geometric *o*'s in *Étoile* and *Nord* are almost symmetrically placed, create a visual triangle with the star, and bring the viewer's eye back from the deep perspective space to the typography.

The experiments in visualization of movement by painters Giacomo Balla in *Dynamism of a Dog on a Leash* and Marcel Duchamp in *Nude Descending a Staircase* (see Chapter 1) are translated and refined by Cassandre in the *L. M. S. Bestway* poster. The train wheels are drawn as graphic abstractions, with the changes in tone reflecting their movement. The typography is also a graphic abstraction of the letterforms. Only a fine outline of detail and shadow in motion are used to create the typography, which indicates the afterimage of swift movement. In both the typography and image a minimum of information is given to the viewer for interpretation, an approach that has two functions: First, it eliminates all superfluous information by focusing on the most important elements, and second, it catches the viewer's eye and attention as the interpretation is made.

Again, the use of the circle and, in this poster, a series of circles help guide the viewer's eye. The "Best Way" typography contributes to closure and completes the circle of the train wheel. The circles in the train wheel drawing are almost overwhelming in attracting the viewer's attention. However, the typography is able to effectively compete for attention because of the three outline-circle periods that follow the L. M. S. initials.

Modern Abstracted Typography

Art nouveau and the movements that were part of it provided a catalyst for the rapid changes and new ideas that were brought to art and design early in the twentieth century. The later movements of cubism, Futurism, suprematism, de Stijl, and constructivism all made individual and collective contributions. During this rapid series of fine and applied art movements, typography responded to the same philosophies, experiments, and influences.

The visual design experiments of the early twentieth century were synthesized at the Bauhaus. It was here that the functional role of typography became accepted doctrine and that the historicism, romanticism, and expressionism of the past found their places in history. At the Bauhaus, architects, artists, and printers in collaboration brought together the tradition and history of visual theory and systemized practice, which helped solidify and develop the emerging profession of graphic design. The result was a new specialization largely independent of its creators. The professions of artist, graphic designer, architect, photographer, and illustrator diverged and developed independently, not codependently as before. But this separation caused each professions to lose some of the power, input, and influence they had collectively gathered and encouraged in graphic design.

Every period of rapid and dramatic change in society, art, and design seems to be followed by a period of relative calm and stasis as artists, designers, and society seek to come to terms with change. In graphic design the period of time from World War II to the 1960s can be seen as a time of both development and stagnation during which change came slowly. Innovators during this time still produced revelatory works, but they were less influential and there were far fewer movements of national or international importance.

Many designers, profoundly affected by the war, never regained their collective dynamic and inspiring force. National differences in graphic design diminished, and the graphic design style became both European and international. The functional role of typography as developed by the Bauhaus and de Stijl began to solidify formally and soon emerged as an international style. As advertising became more important, the emphasis during this time was placed on a pictorial style rather than on typography.

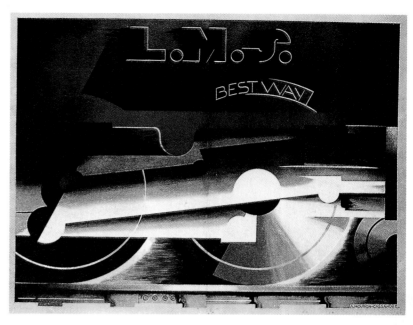

6.11 A. M. Cassandre, *L. M. S. Bestway* poster, 1929. From the collection of Merrill C. Berman, New York City.

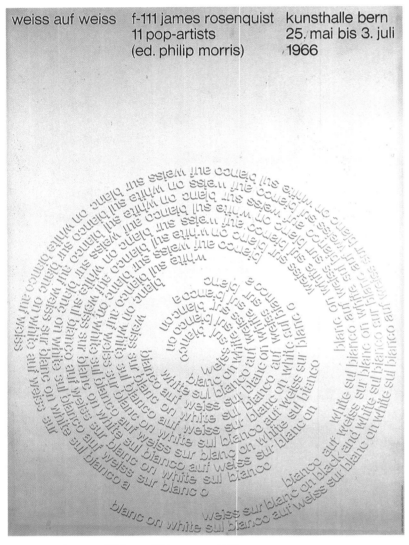

weiss auf weiss f-111 james rosenquist kunsthalle bern
11 pop-artists   25. mai bis 3. juli
(ed. philip morris)   1966

6.12 Peter Megert, *White on White* poster, 1966.

Experimental abstracted typography began to be revised frequently beginning in the mid-1960s. This time also began a period of social change and questioning of traditional values. The formal investigation and organization of set type had become stagnated, and designers again turned to the creative potential of expressionism for visual communication.

Typography can be abstracted in a variety of ways. The only common quality in the works shown in this chapter is that the words' specific verbal meaning is subordinated to the typography's visual connotations. All of the works use traditional typeset letterforms as a basis for nonrepresentational treatment that enhances meaning through color or texture, stylization, addition or subtraction, or inventive design innovation. The resulting compositions are amplified by their suggestive and expressive visual form at the same time that they retain their verbal communication.

Peter Megert's *White on White* poster was for a major exhibition of monochrome art, Weiss auf Weiss, "White on White" **(Fig. 6.12)**. The poster is printed in two colors: blue at the top for the names, dates, and place of two exhibitions and silver for the type image. The abstraction is in the color and the spiraling typography, as only the shadows of the helvetica characters are printed in silver ink. The visual effect is a subtle change in texture from the matte finish of the paper to the glossy finish of the ink. Depending on the lighting conditions and position of the viewer, the typography is invisible or visible by reflected light, thereby making the composition kinetic. The type is repeated in the spiral in different languages: "blanc on white sul bianco auf weiss sur blanc." Hidden in the spiral of typography are the words *black and white* as a tribute to the museum director's fondness for a particular brand of whiskey.

Armin Hofmann reduced, combined, and abstracted two letterforms to create a poster for the work of sculptor David Smith and graphic artist Horst Janssen **(Fig. 6.13)**. The *s* and *j* letterforms are combined through positive and negative space; the *s* as black and the *j* as an outline. The combination occurs in the transition of the curve of the *s* to the vertical stroke of the *j*. Combination and meeting are emphasized as the s is cropped and the terminal stroke becomes the dot for the lowercase *j*. The square in the upper right corner also serves as the composition's starting point for the viewer's eye. Closure helps the viewer complete and identify both letters.

6.13 Armin Hofmann, *David Smith, Horst Janssen* exhibition poster, 1966.

Together these two letterforms make a statement about the relationship between graphic art and sculpture, as they share common shapes and congruent aspects.

Just as the work of the futurists and constructivists reflected in their design of type the developing machine age in the early twentieth century, so too does Wim Crouwel's *Vorm Gevers* (Form Givers) poster reflect the developing computer age **(Fig. 6.14)**. The characters are composed in a manner similar to the rectilinear letterpress element construction of de Stijl. In 1968 the rectangles have new meanings associated with the computer age and are the radiated forms of the liquid crystal display (LCD) screen. The matrix grid is a part of the composition and permits the viewer to see in large scale the organizational structure and construction of the letterforms. Positive and negative space are illustrated as the two most readily accessed display modes of the LCD. The poster was for an exhibition of the work of industrial designers and was prophetic in the way it alludes to the computer.

6.14 Wim Crouwel, *Vorm Gevers* exhibition poster, 1968.

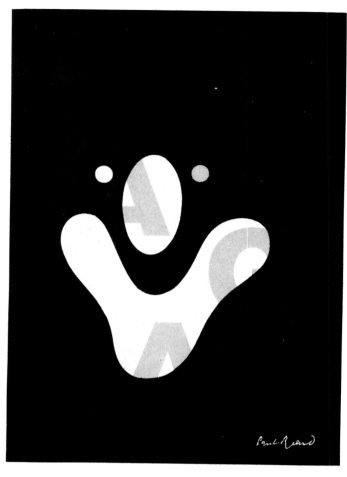

6.15 Paul Rand, *AIGA* poster, 1968.

6.16 Seymour Chwast, *Artone "a,"* 1970.

The visual image of Paul Rand's *AIGA* poster is created only in part by the cropped letterforms **(Fig. 6.15)**. The image is contained in the negative spaces that form the clown's face. Each letter's position is carefully controlled to reveal the part of the symbol that assists in recognition. The crossbar of the first *A* is revealed as an unmistakable clue, and so it is not necessary to be as explicit with the second *A*. A small portion of the horizontal stroke of the *G* is shown so as to avoid confusion with other circular letters. The smallest visual clue is the dot of the *i* that fills one of the eyes of the face, as the dot alone gives the character its identity. The combination of the mask and the cropped letterforms permits the designer to create an image and its connotations from the letterforms and their meaning.

Ordinary india ink was infused with elegance and beauty in Seymour Chwast's package for Artone india ink **(Fig. 6.16)**. The *a* serves a dual purpose as both an identity for the manufacturer and an image of the product. The flowing curves and swelling contrasts of the letterform express the smooth fluid qualities of the product. The stylized *a* has a liquid quality, and the extra bold weight implies the denseness of of india ink's color. The simplicity and appropriateness of the letterform make it an elegant statement about the product.

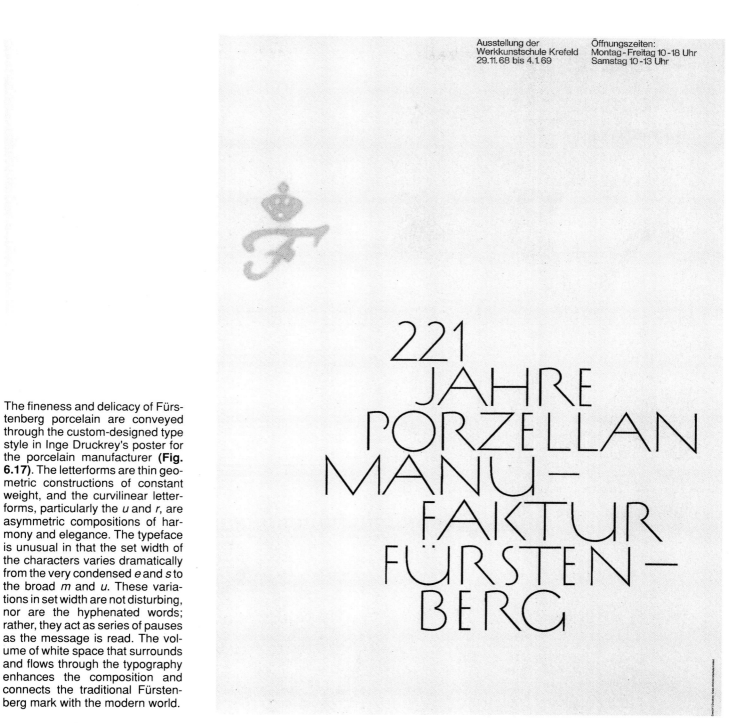

221
JAHRE
PORZELLAN
MANU —
FAKTUR
FÜRSTEN —
BERG

The fineness and delicacy of Fürstenberg porcelain are conveyed through the custom-designed type style in Inge Druckrey's poster for the porcelain manufacturer **(Fig. 6.17)**. The letterforms are thin geometric constructions of constant weight, and the curvilinear letterforms, particularly the *u* and *r,* are asymmetric compositions of harmony and elegance. The typeface is unusual in that the set width of the characters varies dramatically from the very condensed *e* and *s* to the broad *m* and *u.* These variations in set width are not disturbing, nor are the hyphenated words; rather, they act as series of pauses as the message is read. The volume of white space that surrounds and flows through the typography enhances the composition and connects the traditional Fürstenberg mark with the modern world.

6.17 Inge Druckrey, *221 Years Fürstenberg Porcelain* exhibition poster, 1970.

6.18 Herb Lubalin, '72 It's a Great Year..., 1972.

Herb Lubalin is able to see typographic potential from all angles in his work. In his 1972 greeting, "It's a great year,/Anyway you look at it," he plays on the similarities of form in the numbers to create a composition that reads both right side up and upside down **(Fig. 6.18)**. The numbers are playfully composed of stylized excessive contrasts in the thicks, thins, and serifs. The bulbous '72 is further contrasted with simple, fine-line Futura Light type.

Ruedi Rüegg's typographic ballet posters achieve meaning and visual experience through his treatment of the letterforms, words, lines, and composition **(Fig. 6.19)**. In the poster for the Zurich Ballet, a bold sans serif helvetica e rises and leaves the ancient stone cutters' letterforms. The new and modern are connected yet redefined from the traditional. The lines of copy flow across the poster format like dancers on a stage.

The *Ballet Contemporains* poster uses a seemingly ordinary typography to evoke ballet and music through color change **(Fig. 6.20)**. The background is a dense black and the typography a deep blue, creating a minimal contrast in color. However, all of the *a*'s are reversed out in white, creating an asymmetric pattern throughout the page. In this pattern the stops and starts, pauses, and areas of delicacy and intensity cause the viewer's eye to dance on the poster, as will the ballet dancers on the stage.

Rosmarie Tissi's *Englersatz AG* poster for a type house compares and combines serif and sans serif letterforms **(Fig. 6.21)**. The contrast of the *E* in the composition is stunning, juxtaposing the traditional serif character juxtaposed with a modern sans serif character. The grid lines orient the viewer to the differences in the vertical stroke width, the length of the crossbars, and the serif/sans serif configuration. The contrast is again repeated in the uppercase *E* to the lowercase *e*. These contrasts are highlighted with color changes that make the visual statement forceful and dynamic.

6.19 Ruedi Rüegg, *Zurich Ballet* poster, 1972.

6.20 Ruedi Rüegg, *Ballet Contemporains* poster, 1972.

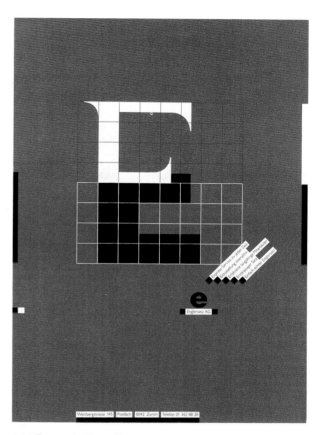

6.21 Rosmarie Tissi, *Englersatz AG* poster, 1983.

6.22 Don Grimes, *San Antonio* typography, 1983.

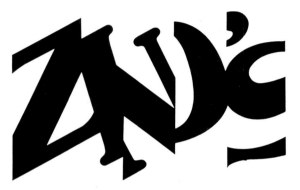

6.23 Stan Brod, *Zino's Restaurant* identity, 1983.

Don Grimes abstracted the typography to a few drawn strokes in *San Antonio* **(Fig. 6.22)**. The baseline and cap height indications as well as the letterform strokes convey the quality of guidelines for an architectural sketch. The strokes also have the feeling of precise rapid movement. Closure is used to complete the visual clues in the viewer's mind. This typography highlights the geometry of the letterforms and those areas of the characters that are necessary for recognition, such as the diagonals of the *A* and *N*, the crossbar of the *T,* and circles of the *S* and *O*.

Many letterforms can be almost 75 percent cropped and still be legible; the key is to crop selectively in a way that retains important visual clues. Stan Brod used this selective cropping technique in his identity for Zino's Restaurant **(Fig. 6.23)**. The letterforms tilt in space and meet to form a single image, word, and identity. The eye rapidly determines what portions of the letterforms have been retained and explores the new shapes that are created as they touch.

Unconventional in her approach, Margo Chase uses illustration, pattern, color, texture, and decoration to set her typographic work apart from others. The typography of *Eleanor, Jungle Wave* album cover and *Steven Wright* logo are illustrated abstracted typography **(Figs. 6.24, 6.25)**. The construction of the letterforms is based on the proportions of traditional condensed type styles and is decoratively abstracted within a single visual language to become identities. *Stephen Wright* uses repetitive line weights and decorations as well as a top and bottom holding rule. *Eleanor, Jungle Wave* introduces a zigzag line that is repeated in the strokes of "Eleanor" and less decoratively in "Jungle Wave." Each has an irregular, hand-drawn feel, and the lack of rigid geometry is a delightful departure from set type.

6.24 Margo Chase, *Eleanor, Jungle Wave* logo for album cover, 1986. Warner Bros. Records.

6.25 Margo Chase, *Steven Wright* logo for album cover, 1986. Warner Bros. Records.

6.26 Margo Chase, *Kathy Guild* personal logo, 1987.

6.27 Margo Chase, *New Product Guide* cover design for *Computer Reseller Magazine* special issue, 1987.

Pattern and texture also are important to the *Kathy Guild* personal logo and in the *New Product Guide* cover **(Figs. 6.26, 6.27)**. The abstracted typography becomes a surface through which patterns of geometric shapes further abstract the letterforms. The *New Product Guide* cover is more conventional in that the letterforms seem to be rigidly geometric. However, they are abstracted with expansion, condensation, decoration, faceting, and the introduction of color changes. Decorative elements of dots, squares, and triangles separate the words and are rhythmic devices that lead the eye through the composition. Additional decorations appear in the interior portions of some of the letterforms and enhance the vertical stress of the word *Product*. The decoration in this composition works with the letterforms to become a part of the typography.

It is unusual to find abstracted typography in package design, as most clients are primarily concerned that their product be able to compete with similar products. This attitude usually results in diluted design solutions that vary in color but rarely in form. But the packaging design for Sparkling Ribena black currant juice drink, by Blackburn's Ltd., breaks away from this attitude and beautifully departs from some of the usual rules of food packaging **(Fig. 6.28)**. The color black is normally avoided in food packaging as unappetizing, but in *Sparkling Ribena* it plays on the "black" currant flavor and is a color enhancer that causes the magenta and red in the typography to glow. The abstracted and fragmented typestyle of the word *Ribena* is unlike any other used for a soft drink, and it sets the product apart on visually polluted store shelves. The counters of the type have been pulled out and enhanced by a change in color and compositional space. These counters join other geometric shapes that allude to the carbonated, "sparkling" quality of the product.

6.28 John Blackburn, art director, Don Williams, designer, *Sparkling Ribena* package, 1987. Blackburn's Ltd.

6.29 Rudy VanderLans, design, Nigel Grierson, photographer, cover for *Emigre 9*, 1988.

6.30 Rudy VanderLans, opening page for *Emigre 9*, 1988.

Rudy VanderLans and Zuzana Licko explored and developed the potential that the Macintosh computer has brought to typography and typographic composition. Both VanderLans and Licko were born and educated in Europe and are now working in Berkeley, California. They brought with them the contemporary Dutch striving toward innovation by refusing to be limited by tradition. Vanderlans is both the art director and publisher for *Emigre* magazine, "The Magazine That Ignores Boundaries." With his design associate and wife, Zuzana Licko, they have designed typefaces and compositions without precedent.

In VanderLans's and Licko's work it can be seen more than ever before that the designer is in control of all aspects of typography. The computer offers the designer almost complete control and the possibility of varying at will the major design elements of column positions, widths, and shapes. The leading, word space, and letter space of the lines, words, and characters also are ultimately flexible and can be changed with only a few keystrokes. This flexibility and control extend even to the individual letterform, which can be customized or kerned individually. The result is a composition of customized detailing, shape, space, and texture, as well as communication of meaning.

The cover and title page of *Emigre 9* introduces the viewer to a highly abstracted custom typestyle that explores the pixelated character of computer composition **(Figs. 6.29, 6.30)**. The display-size letterforms on the cover were composed on the computer with blocks of pixels. Thicks and thins are functionally and aesthetically used in a variable configuration to suite the needs of a particular character or location. The letterforms use essentially a sans serif type style, with serif characters introduced as needed to increase legibility or to add emphasis. The weight of the letterforms varies as does the compositional architecture, to suit the particular position of the letter in a word and/or the aesthetic eye of the designer.

The interior opening page features a similar pixelated display type, named Oakland Syx, in a version designed by Licko that has been standardized for text. This typeface uses all uppercase characters widely letter spaced and leaded to increase readability and to create a graphic texture on the page. This bold and airy texture is contrasted to the "Introduction" column that is typeset in another face of much smaller size and leaded more tightly for a denser, more intense texture. The composition of the page is a fluid play of white space and textural elements.

An interior spread of *Emigre 9* reveals that the same compositional style and objectives are pursued throughout the magazine **(Fig. 6.31)**. Different portions of the article are separated into columns. Each column has its own texture and shape, giving it an individual identity and compositional space. The page numbers are in the body of the page and are offset by bold rules and bold type. Images are handled in the same way as text is, in that they both are treated as elements of composition and communication.

6.31 Rudy VanderLans, page from *Emigre 9*, 1988.

6.32 Rudy VanderLans, design, Wim Crouwel and Zuzana Licko, typography, title page for *Emigre 8*, 1988.

variex iſ a ſtroke poſtſcript typeface conſtructed from lineſ of uniform weight. theſe letterformſ have been reduced to the baſic powerful geſtureſ of primitive writing handſ. the alphabet iſ ſingle-caſe with alternative characterſ for optimal letter combinationſ. the bold iſ three timeſ the weight of the light which iſ half the weight of the regular. {a ratio of 1:2:3}

aAbcdefgHijkLMN
opdqrſtuvwxyz
How doeſ one become an emigre?

aAbcdefgHijkLMN
opdqrſtuvwxyz
How doeſ one become an emigre?

aAbcdefgHijkLMN
opdqrſtuvwxyz
How doeſ one become an emigre?

6.33 Zuzana Licko, Variex typeface, 1988.

Many of the traditional rules of publication design are broken in *Emigre*. These rules argue that for readability, publications should have regularized grid systems and a standard style, position, and placement of elements such as titles and page numbers. Interestingly, *Emigre's* flexible grid style creates its own visual rhythm and reader anticipation, and what little is lost in readability is more than gained in visual interest.

The title page of *Emigre 8* demonstrates some of the computer's abstraction and composition capabilities **(Fig. 6.32)**. The minimally reduced typeface for the word *alienation* is composed with horizontal and vertical strokes of computer composition. No curvilinear or diagonal strokes are used, except in the edge transitions from horizontal to vertical strokes. The small, saw-toothed edges of pixel composition are left in the large *8* as they give a texture to the number. The pronunciation guide reversed out of an ellipse provides another clue to help the viewer translate the highly abstracted letterforms in *alienation*.

Zuzana Licko designed the Variex typeface out of simple geometric shapes specifically for the computer **(Fig. 6.33)**. The face is of singlecase construction, without uppercase and lowercase, and does not have an x-height. Licko described Variex as follows: "Variex is a stroke postscript typeface constructed from lines of uniform weight. These letterforms have been reduced to the basic powerful gestures of primitive writing hands. the alphabet is singlecase with alternative characters for optimal letter combinations. The bold is three times the weight of the light which is half the weight of the regular." This typeface provides for the variability of the computer in selecting the style of the letterform in regard to those that surround it. The three font changes of light, regular, and bold read well as text and display types. Singlecase construction is an idea that was originally presented at the Bauhaus by Herbert Bayer and perhaps now, in Variex, is a reality.

Selective cropping of the typography creates an interesting composition of light and dark in the poster for Octavo by the collaborative firm, Eight Five Zero **(Fig. 6.34)**. The bold letterforms and numbers are abstracted by the selective removal of sections of their strokes, and the removed sections guide the viewer's eye horizontally and then vertically to the columns of text. Each of the bold numbers represents a past issue of Octavo, the most current issue is largest, and the light small regular numbers a future issue. The weights of the columns of type have a similar weight change as the boldest column discusses the most recent issue.

6.34 Eight Five Zero, *Octavo Journal* poster for Eight Five Zero Publishing, 1988.

Experimental
Abstracted Typography

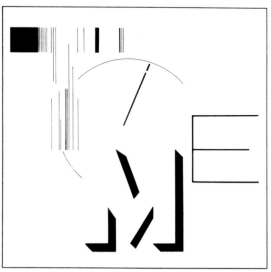

6.A Greg Thomas, instructor, student designer, *R* Letterform Study, California Institute of the Arts, 1977/78.

6.B Greg Thomas, instructor, student designer, *E* Letterform Study, California Institute of the Arts, 1977/78.

6.C Greg Thomas, instructor, student designer, *Time* composition, California Institute of the Arts, 1977/78.

Student work is experimental and emphasizes innovation particularly in the realm of abstracted typography. Such work forces the designer to put aside momentarily function and problem solving as the primary purpose of graphic design. Instead, the designer returns to the early nineteenth- and twentieth-century beginnings of design as purely a means of expression.

Greg Thomas, a graphic designer and design educator, conducts experimental investigations of letterforms in his basic typography courses. The *R* Letterform Study compares and contrasts the shape and weight of the strokes **(Fig. 6.A)**. The uppercase *R* is reduced to a single fine line of a curve and a diagonal stroke. The lowercase *r* contains both a thick vertical line and a thin curved stroke. The combination of uppercase and lowercase strokes of a constant weight result in a new visual sign for *R*.

The relationships between an Old Style and a contemporary typeface are investigated in the *E* Letterform Study **(Fig. 6.B)**. Only vertical strokes are used for visual definition, permitting the viewer to complete the letterform through closure. The short vertical strokes in the contemporary version act as serifs in identifying the shape.

The *Time* composition expresses some of the visual qualities of the concept of time through the abstracted typography **(Fig. 6.C)**. The irregular rhythm of the strokes that compose the *T* suggest faster and shorter intervals of time. The *i* is both a letterform and the hand of a clock that measures time. The *M* is identified in shadow only, perhaps suggesting the elusiveness of time. Finally, the *E* is extended, alluding to the stretching out of time. Many different ideas and concepts of time are expressed through abstracted typography.

The letterform manipulation series directed by graphic designer and design educator Bill Deere is an experimental Basic Typography project **(Figs. 6.D)**. The objectives of the exercise are to expose students to some of the possibilities of visual expression inherent within a specific letterform, and examine the degree of legibility and resilience of a particular type family.

Each student works with an uppercase or lowercase letterform from one of the five basic type divisions. After examining the structural characteristics of individual letterforms, students choose the method of fragmentation: horizontal, vertical, diagonal, or circular line matrix. The letterform is cut at intervals on the selected matrix and shifted.

The results of the exercise are then analyzed. When objects as familiar as letterforms are distorted through manipulation, the viewer's eye conducts its own visual investigation of form in order to decipher the puzzle. Because of this visual investigation, the manipulated letterforms attract considerably more attention than untouched typeset letterforms. It is found that some of the manipulated letterforms appear bent and seem to become dimensional as they shift or waver in space. Serif letterforms retain their character as letterforms more strongly under excessive manipulation than do sans serif letterforms, because of the additional visual identity clues of serifs. Visual connotations of the letterforms are energetic and can include speed, violence, distortion, melting, and shattering.

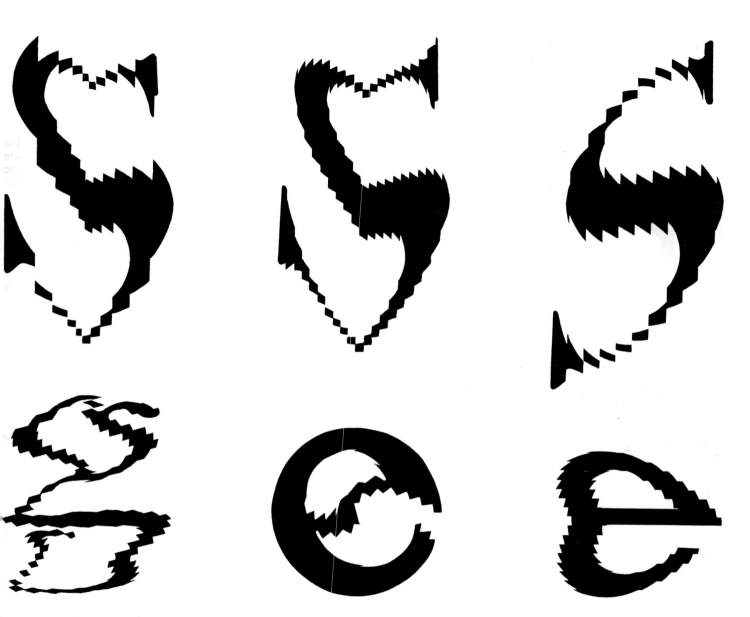

6.D (series of 6) Bill Deere, instructor, Win Utermohlen, designer, *e* series; Sabine Moore, designer, *s* series; Melissa Graham, designer, *g* series; Letterform Manipulation Series, North Carolina State University, Department of Product and Visual Design, 1988.

GNUES

GNUES

GNUES

6.E (series of 3) Bill Deere, instructor, Seunghee Suhr, designer, *Gnues* Subtractive/Additive Investigation, North Carolina State University, Department of Product and Visual Design, 1988.

Lyrehc

Lyrehc

Lyrehc

6.F (series of 3) Bill Deere, instructor, Cheryl Paulin, designer, *Lyrehc* Subtractive/Additive Investigation, North Carolina State University, Department of Product and Visual Design, 1988.

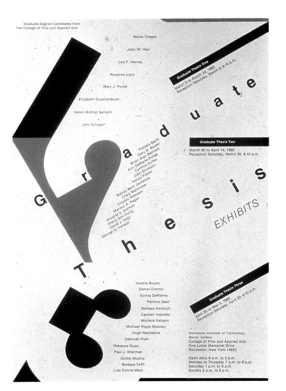

6.G R. Roger Remington, instructor, John B. Malinoski, designer, *Graduate Thesis* poster, Rochester Institute of Technology, 1985.

The Subtractive/Additive Investigation series is an Advanced Typography project directed by Bill Deere. In this course and exercise students build on their experiences with letterform manipulation. The objectives are to experimentally investigate the visual connotations of form that are potentially possible by subtracting or adding elements to the letterforms that compose a word **(Figs. 6.E, 6.F)**.

Students use the letters in their name but spell it backwards to prevent any semantic association between the form manipulation and their name. Words are typeset in classic typefaces and students are encouraged to work as experimentally as possible while retaining legibility. The number of variations possible are infinite, therefore students are encouraged to work systematically. After subtracting or adding elements from or to the word the opposite situation is then applied. Finally, students select the most interesting and/or successful solutions for presentation and discussion.

The results of the project reveal a variety of expressive visual connotations. In any type of letterform manipulation the viewer's eye constantly seeks meaning. These implied meanings, or visual connotations, depend on the viewer's range of experience and imagination. The *Lyrehc* series revealed connotations of confetti and happiness, danger and sharpness, music and fabric, and wear and scratching. The *Gnues* word revealed connotations of clouds and bullet holes, ink spots and paint, hiding and irregularity, and chopping.

6.H (series of 5) Katherine McCoy, instructor, Robert Nakata, designer, *Heinz Ketchup* Vernacular Message Sequence, Cranbrook Academy of Art, 1985.

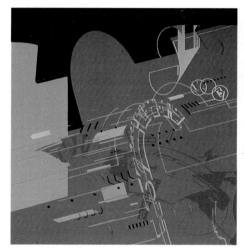
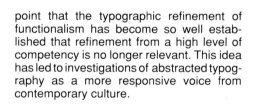
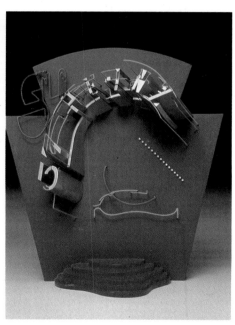

John B. Malinoski's poster for three graduate thesis shows uses numbers and contrasting diagonals to organize the information presented **(Fig. 6.G)**. The numbers are emphasized by figure ground reversal, whereby visual ambiguity is created by a fluctuating dominance of the negative and positive spaces. The names of the participants of each show are tailored to become an edge of each number, which reinforces the positive space of the numbers in conflict with the bold negative spaces. The negative spaces change in color, connect, and bring the eye down the page. The numbers function as organization for the information as well as visual and perceptual indications of the fresh and innovative work presented in the exhibitions.

Katherine McCoy's career-long interest in typography resulted from her dual role as both a professional graphic design consultant and a design educator. Her current interest in typography stems from the view-point that the typographic refinement of functionalism has become so well established that refinement from a high level of competency is no longer relevant. This idea has led to investigations of abstracted typography as a more responsive voice from contemporary culture.

The Vernacular Message Sequence explores the multiple interpretations of common and traditional words, phrases, or communication elements of modern culture **(Figs. 6.H** through **6.J)**. These interpretations can include alternative meanings, alternative orders, and various visual interpretations. In this experimental process the message undergoes a visual transformation through which communication and meaning are subordinated to graphic form.

The *Heinz Ketchup* series also follow a pattern of abstraction that is fully developed in a color study and a three-dimensional sculpture **(Figs. 6.H)**. Translations in color and dimensional form yield a new visual vocabulary of compositional qualities. Compositions that were begun as experimental graphic design have, through graphic abstraction, led to work that is more congruent with the objectives of art than those of design.

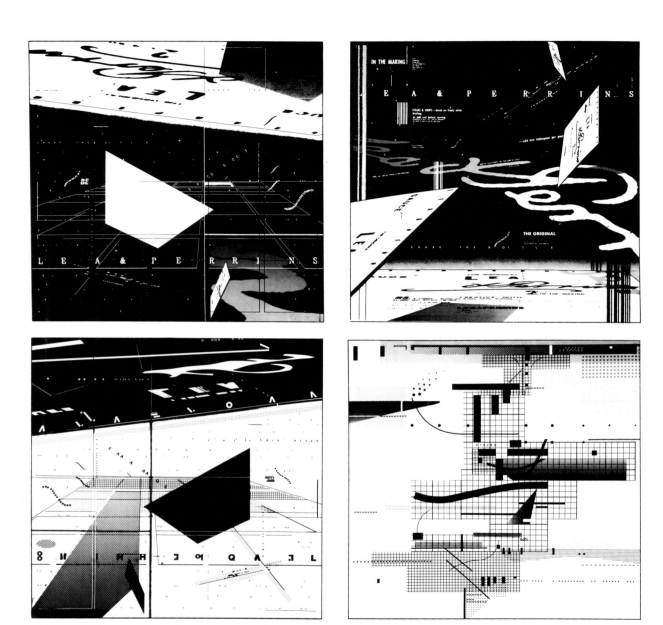

6.I (series of 4) Katherine McCoy, instructor, Mark Tweed, designer, *Lea & Perrins* Vernacular Message Sequence, Cranbrook Academy of Art, 1983.

The *Lea & Perrins* Vernacular Message Sequence begins with the rearrangement of all typography, including UPC codes and ingredients **(Figs. 6.I)**. All type is used in its actual size and freely composed so as to investigate combinations of form and meaning. This composition is followed by experimentation with typographic abstractions of typography and compositional arrangement. Subsequent compositions reduce the typographic elements even further to abstract forms of rhythm and texture.

The *Kowtow* compositions explore the journey of a word to image sequence **(Figs. 6.J)**. The series was designed manually on the computer and the designer, graduate graphic design student Allen Hori, developed this idea as a comment on his early attitude toward the computer, that he was required to bow down to it (he has since become a convert). The word "kowtow" undertakes the gradual transformation from verbal to abstract to visual meaning.

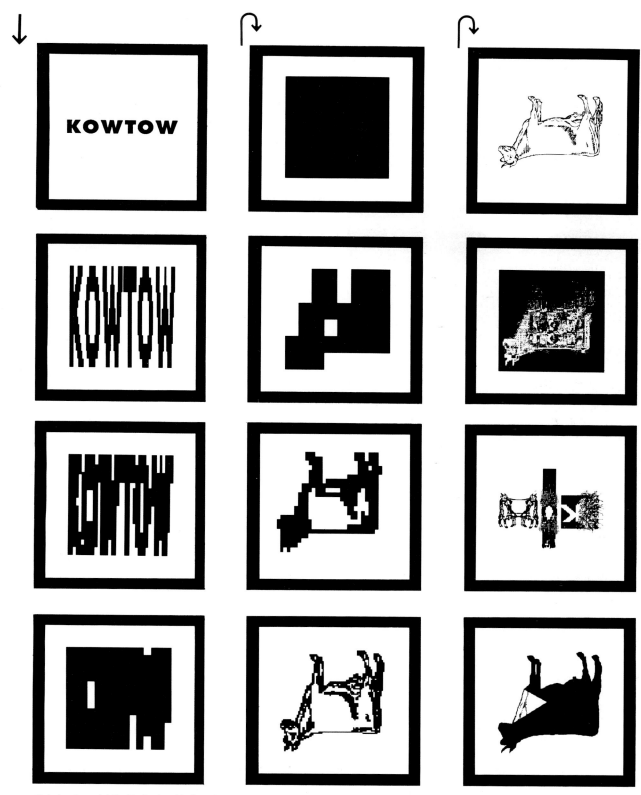

6.J (series of 12) Katherine McCoy, instructor, Allen Hori, designer, *Kowtow* Word-to-Image Sequence, Cranbrook Academy of Art, 1988.

Index

Printing:
Arcata Graphics/Kingsport Press

Binding:
Arcata Graphics/Kingsport Press

Layout and Production:
Aldus Pagemaker 3.01 software
Macintosh II computer

Typography:
Harlan Type
Columbus, Ohio
9/10 Helvetica with 12/12 Helvetica Bold Titles
set on the Linotron 300 Digital Typesetter

Design:
Kimberly Elam